LIFE'S JOURNEY: W

BY,

STEPHANNETH P. ADAMS

THIS BOOK IS PRESENTED TO:

_____

FROM:

_____

ON:

_____

MAY YOU FIND JOY AND PEACE AS YOU
DISCOVER WHO YOU ARE AS A WOMAN.

LIFE'S JOURNEY: WOMAN TO WOMAN

STEPHANNETH P. ADAMS

ACKNOWLEDGEMENTS

Thank you to everyone who believes in my gifts. Your support means more than you will ever know!
Thank you to God, My Lord, and Savior.
Lastly, thank you for purchasing this book. You are stronger than you think!

TABLE OF CONTENTS

PRAYER FOR THE WOMAN

A NOTE FROM THE AUTHOR

A WOMAN'S STRUGGLE THROUGH LIFE

A WOMAN'S PREPARATION FOR LOVE

A WOMAN'S INSPIRATION FOR LIFE

MEET THE AUTHOR

MY NOTE PAD

PRAYER FOR THE WOMAN

Dear Lord,

My prayer is that You speak to every woman (man) who opens the pages of this book. Move her (him) away from any feelings of shame and failure. Instead, transform her feelings into those of love and acceptance. Forgive her where she has made mistakes. Heal her where she is hurting. Make her beautiful where she feels ugly. Fix her where she is broken. If she is apprehensive to believe in You, I ask that You understand. Open her heart to Your voice and clearly speak to her through the written words of each page. May she and I become the best of sisters as we share in the journey of our struggles and experience Your transforming power. In Jesus' name.

DIRECTIONS

Please spend time going through this journey as the book takes you through a personalized transformative journey. Take your time as you meditate and complete the life's scriptures, points to ponder, chapter challenges, and share your growth with other women. Completing the first few chapters may take some time. That is okay, keep going. I honestly want you to heal from your past before moving into love and purpose.

A NOTE FROM THE AUTHOR

There is a dire need to share with you the story of how this book began. By revealing one of my most vulnerable moments in life, I will allow the veil of the woman behind the cover of this book to become unleashed. The failures of my life's journey will be portrayed through stories, poems, and quotes. Not only will I share personal stories, but stories of women I met throughout life. These writings will expose you to personal growth strategies, biblical truth, and inspiration.

Let's begin the journey. In 2007 I began to record my most intimate feelings about life. At the time my life was filled with confusion, doubt, regret, and quite frankly, failure. At least for me I considered my life to be a depiction of failed dreams. I remember around 2006 I experienced my first heartbreak and my most intimate moments with God. My heart was shattered. I felt used, stupid, crazy, and most of all confused. The confusion led me to get frank with God. Him and I needed to have a "heated" conversation, if you will. It was a conversation between, as Beyoncé' puts it, "me, myself, and I". Instead of the I, I inserted God. We needed to talk. It's weird having a conversation with myself and God, right?

However, you have no idea how much I needed that conversation. I literally was on the brink of determining whether my life would go forward, backwards, or stay stagnant. At that time my internal struggle was for real! In my eyes time was passing by quickly. I mean, I was 21. There was no way that I could not have figured out what career I wanted, whom I would marry, where I would live, and who I was. Trust me, knowing what I know in 2019, I would have told myself to take a huge "chill pill". So many times, in our younger years we want everything fast and easy. Having to endure a growth process is almost unheard of, especially as a millennial.

Anyway, at that moment I was in dire need to understand the purpose of my life. Something that never seems to go away with age. I needed to know that God was seeing how my life was unfolding. I mean, did He care that the guy misused me? Did He not see my friends stab me in the back? Did He not see that everyone wanted me to become a medical doctor when I thought that I should become a pastor? Where was God? Why was He not fixing everything? Geeze! Then, there was the, "why me?", that we ask every time that we encounter a tragic moment.

A conversation with God was what I needed. The conversation began as I prostrated myself on my bedroom floor. If I recall, I was not able to sleep the night before and woke up in excruciating emotional pain. I walked into my parents' bedroom crying that morning. I remember my dad saying something like, "Stephanneth, I know that we are your parents, but this time there is nothing that we can do for you. This time you're going to have to take it to God". Wow! Those words hit like a ton of bricks because for the first time I realized that I was becoming a woman. My parents would not be able to solve my life's issues. They were humans like me. Emotional pain was not something that they could heal. This time it was time to put on my big girl panties and hash things out with God. After my dad spoke, I remember both of my parents hugging me, saying a prayer, and allowing me to go back into my room with a broken heart.

Believing that God's presence inhabited the confines of my bedroom, I began to speak. My face had a look of contemplation. I desperately needed guidance to find a way out of my bad circumstances. A way out of this pain. Emotions of despair and failure were crowding my mind. I spoke, "God, I thought my life was heading for success and now it has taken a different course?" Why were my dreams fading like quicksand in the palm of my hands? Pondering over these questions struck my heart with grief. Why was God allowing me to go through what I thought was the hardest time of my life? I guess at age 21 I didn't realize that life would bring more hard times.

I wondered if God was okay with me questioning His plan for my life. Was He okay with me telling Him how I really felt? Yet, I continued the conversation. He needed a piece of my mind and to feel my pain. "Lord, even though I'm not at the spiritual or socioeconomic level that I desire to be in life, I am working towards getting there. It's not easy getting there and I don't know how" (my ex at that time told everyone that, "I did not have my stuff together and he needed a girl that did"). Ugh, somehow those words were too superficial for me. I needed words that expressed my anger to God. God needed to know what was deep inside my soul. I spoke again with a conviction that I was going to let God have it! "Lord, as I look over my life, I realize that getting to a place of satisfaction is taking longer than I expected. My love life is not working out, my career is on the brink of failure, and my dreams are fading. I feel disgusted. I feel busted. My pathway is not clear."

That's it! Those were the words that I needed. Let me give you, the reader, a little background on what was happening in my life. In 2002 I began college as a pre-medical student. I was unsure if a medical profession was what I wanted for a career choice. During my junior year, I realized that my only passion was not medicine. In fact, it was not my main passion at all and remains as such. Deep within, I have always had a passion to speak. A passion to inspire. Counseling, healthcare, writing, travel, and dance bring me great joy. The problem at the time (even now) was that I had (have) no clue how each of these passions would (will) mesh together as one purpose. I wondered if God could make all my desires come true. Quite frankly, I wanted God to fix everything the way that I wanted, how I wanted, and to do it quickly. Discovering what were my passions wasn't an easy process. Can you relate? Even as adults we still don't figure it out. Some of us never do.

There were times that I had to pray and ask God for direct guidance. I felt a calling to enter ministry, but I had a love for the sciences. I was good at science. Finding a way to blend these two callings together was very stressful. A career in the medical field would financially support me and make my parents proud. You see, my dad is a physician (M.D.), a surgeon at that! Everyone expected me to matriculate into medical school to prove that I was just as smart as him. Anything other than that was second to none, or a means of settling for less. At least that is what family members and others proved by their statements and actions. Can you pause for a second to think about whether you have spent your whole life trying to find approval from your parents, friends, co-workers, or other people? Not just through a degree, but in your salary, the house you bought, clothes that you wear, in the way you raise your children, or in the spouse you chose?

Well, at the time I believed that ministry brought me such satisfaction, but my heart needed the approval of my surroundings, something I've had to grapple with as I grew into a woman. Not to mention, I did not see how ministry could sustain my finances, something my dad made me think about. He always said, "well, what type of life do you want to live?". Looking back, it was good advice. Someway and somehow, I needed to find a way to blend my passions together and reap the benefits. I thought, "clearly, God is not going to do it, so I need to figure it out." It wasn't until I fervently prayed for God's direction that I felt led to the perfect pathway. This would mean that I would have to let go of all my plans, allow God to re-route my entire direction, move to far-away places, accept rejection, remain in solitude, and most of all make changes. I would have to trust God.

When the re-routing began, I was still heart-broken, anxious, afraid, betrayed, talked about, abandoned, and bruised. What I did not realize was that this was only the beginning of real life. I ended up graduating with a B.S. in Biology with which you can't find work, but I believed in the prayer God showed me the profession that would provide me with the tools to utilize my passions. So, I applied to post-baccalaureate programs, approximately 15, thinking that God was getting ready to shine heaven's special light on me. To my dismay, from every school a rejection letter came in the mail. I didn't meet their qualifications. Each rejection was a sign that my life would probably end right there. The rejections caused me to doubt that I correctly understood God's guidance. Despite each rejection I wanted to believe that God would provide me with an opportunity. I felt like quitting and sometimes I still do.

On top of all the rejection letters from these institutions, I was experiencing rejection from the guy whom I loved. My whole life seemed to be centered around the idea that I was worthy of rejection. Everything was linked to the idea of failure which seemed like my only option. I thought that my 21 years of life was a waste of time because I had nothing to prove to others. I was just a 21-year-old girl, living at home, a college graduate without a purpose/job, and the girl who told everyone that she was getting married only to witness him marrying someone else. Yeah, I was that girl with nothing to prove, except my parents' accomplishments. My goals were taking long to become established and my purpose was nowhere in sight. So many questions encapsulated my mind. Where would my life lead? What choices would I make now? Who would I become?

As I laid on the floor, rehashing everything, God spoke, "My thoughts are nothing like your thoughts," says the LORD. "And my ways are far beyond anything you could imagine" (Isaiah 55:8, NLT). God reminded me that He saw the very best in me when I saw the words f-a-i-l-u-r-e written across my forehead. Not everyone saw the best in me and not everyone wanted the best for me. I remember a very close girlfriend of mine at the time who inflicted more pain than comfort. It is amazing how quickly people change or use your failures to overshadow theirs. She and others helped fill me with rejection, crushed my joy, and trampled my dreams. However, I had family members and other people who encouraged me to see myself as God saw me. "So, God created man in His own image, in the image of God He created him; male and female He created them" (Genesis 1:27, NIV).

I remember the day my dad suggested that I fast and pray for guidance and healing. He saw my disappointment and reminded me that he's had his own. My dad reassured me that if he could endure life's ups and downs, then so could I. The key was to allow God to fight my battles. The week I chose to fast and pray was the week that I experienced my first miracle! I was waiting for an answer from the last academic institution. If the opportunity opened, I could begin my academic journey. If it remained closed, I would be further setback. I was a nervous wreck that week.

Later that week my family and I came home from an Adventist Youth Society program. At the time I was a member of the Seventh-Day Adventist Church which was another journey. My family and I entered the kitchen where a huge white envelope laid on the counter. In apprehension for the fear of rejection, I slowly opened the letter. As I began to read it, I could not believe what I was reading. God opened the door. An opportunity to pursue additional baccalaureate studies in nursing was granted. I was finally stepping onto a new path. In that moment, I knew God wanted to reveal His miraculous power to change my circumstances. God wanted to grant me success and love me past the rejection of others.

I realized that God wanted to give me a special sense of serenity when my life wasn't working out the way I wanted. I found that a faithful prayer had the power to change circumstances. What I thought was impossible, God made those things possible. As I continued, my eyes sparkled like diamonds. Something took over my soul and gave me a deep sense of joy. I began speaking, "Every day I see where You have brought me from. Every day I am closer to my destiny. Through these life experiences I have realized one true thing, towards me You have never changed Your unfailing love. Through my downfalls, setbacks, and setups, You have remained faithfully by my side."

In that quiet moment of conversation, I was able to remember every time I questioned God about my purpose, worth, beauty, intelligence, and faith. I watched my enemies prosper as I sank into bouts of depression. I lost a glimpse of hope. To my amazement, still I was given an undeniable faith that reassured me that everything would be okay. Through God's healing power I realized how good He wanted to be to me, His daughter.

God's love made me feel loved when was unlovable. God's beauty flourished inside of me when I felt ugly. God's wisdom made me wise when I was stupid. God's strength made me strong when I was weak. God's power gave me faith to trust Him. Revelation 21:5 NLT reads, "And the one sitting on the throne said, "Look, I am making everything new!" And then he said to me, "Write this down, for what I tell you is trustworthy and true".

Through my intimate conversations with God, I understood that I had journeyed to a place of love. The strength to love and let go was given to me during those moments. No longer could I hold on to the past. I had to let it go. My struggles became my steppingstones. My failures became my purpose. God spoke to me the day I laid on the floor. His final words were, "Stephanneth, it's time to arise and slumber no more. It's time to let go and let Me handle your problems. It's time to be restored and propelled into your destiny." That night changed my life forever. I arose from God's voice and knew that my mission was to encourage other young women who felt the same. That night I arose with words in my heart ready to be expressed from the tip of a pen onto paper. My old life passed away and new life began. That's when this book started.

~Note from The Author Challenge~

As you continue to read the chapters within this book understand that its purpose is to heal. Every word is meaningful and allows my inner being to be transparent to you. Some stories are about my life. Other stories are about other women. I pray that the writings pierce your heart causing you to accept the reality of your life's journey. May you come to the realization that "with God all things are possible". Believe me when I say that God has your best interest at heart.

~Life Scriptures~

"Jesus looked at them and said, "With man this is impossible, but with God all things are possible" (Matthew 19:26).

~Points to Ponder~

- ❖ In your note pad describe some life circumstances that caused you to view yourself as a failure.
- ❖ Has rejection caused you to stop believing in your dreams?
- ❖ Where does your inner strength derive to overcome life's battles?
- ❖ Have you allowed bad circumstances to hinder or help your personal growth?
- ❖ Do you believe God loves you, wants to restore you, and help you become a better woman?

A WOMAN'S STRUGGLE THROUGH LIFE

CHAPTER 1

FROM SHAME TO ACCEPTANCE

I define **shame** as a feeling of disgust. A person filled with shame thinks that they are less than average, guilty, and/or un-worthy of living. There are various circumstances that can lead us to develop a sense of shame. Here are some examples:

- ❖ A failed relationship
- ❖ Divorce
- ❖ Abandonment by parents
- ❖ Teenage pregnancy
- ❖ Rape
- ❖ Loss of virginity
- ❖ Self-hatred
- ❖ Poverty
- ❖ Discrimination
- ❖ Unemployment
- ❖ Lost educational opportunities
- ❖ Assault
- ❖ Loneliness
- ❖ Not knowing your purpose
- ❖ A life-threatening illness
- ❖ A disability

Everywhere people are living their lives in shame. Usually shame latches onto us during our childhood and travels into our younger years. Young adulthood is a time when we begin to reflect on our childhood, past experiences, and current circumstances. It's a time many of us start to judge ourselves to determine how our future will develop. We judge how our adulthood will transpire based on what happened during our childhood.

If our childhood memories involve thoughts of happiness, we are more likely to believe that our future will be brighter. However, when our childhood memories are filled with gloom, doom, bad choices, and circumstances, we believe that our future will reflect failure. Having thoughts of a failing future will cause us to live a life full of shame. It happens to the best of us. We may present smiles to the outside world, but our internal world is a pitfall. Some of us even have, or will die in our shame, never experiencing freedom.

Do you live with shame? If so, you might be trying everything in your power to erase it. A depiction of your current life and future is that of a woman who constantly seeks acceptance from others, pretends to smile, lives a façade, builds emotional walls, and never wants to face your truth. This doesn't sound good, right? I know because I have been there. Not to say that every area of my life was filled with shame, but there were some areas. Let me explain. I grew up in a stable, middle-class (some may say rich), spiritual, and loving home. My family supplied me with wisdom, love, and financial necessities. They are a reason why I am who I am.

However, they were not God. They simply were human beings and possessed no power to fulfill all my voids. As humans they could not solve any of my problems, rather, they could create more. Just like many women, I had voids, issues, feelings, and secrets. I am sure that each of my family members had those very same things. We all do! At the time I wrote this chapter I was twenty-six and lived a life with periodic shameful circumstances, choices, thoughts, and feelings. Some people would look at me and disagree. I concealed my shamefulness like most of us. We harbor negative emotions and bury them deep inside hoping that they never surface. Bad idea!

Reflecting to my teenage years, I remember experiencing overwhelming feelings about what my future would be like. What would I be when I grew up? Would I make my parents happy? (Sis, you will never make anyone happy) Would I get married? Could I have children? What would my life be like? I wanted to know what my purpose was. These thoughts became significant. In my early twenties I desired to find a life-time partner. I was going through the developmental stage of isolation versus intimacy. My family and friends could not be there for me the way they were as a child. Things were different now. Life was changing. I needed to find my purpose, a career, husband, spiritual enlightenment, social stamina, and self-worth.

As I spoke to you in the "Note from The Author", I experienced a failed romantic relationship (since then I've experienced more), rejection from academic institutions, friends, and church members. I lost my sense of self-worth. During my junior year in college, I met a young man whom I believed was destined to be my husband. This thought faded a year and a half after our first date. I learned that who I thought was my future life-time partner and friend, was a human stumbling block causing me to lose focus on God's plan

16

for my life.

I was betrayed by him and a few others whom I believed were close friends. As quickly as we were engaged, we were separated! He ended up marrying a mutual church sister. Two months after our break-up, he and his new wife, came to church flaunting perfectly nestled newlywed rings. I often wondered, "He was the one who cheated on me, lost his spiritual hindsight, messed up his finances, and lost his ambition for academic goals. I came into his life and helped him in all these areas. When I said that I was willing to work through the problems that he created, he told me that he was tired of working it out. He wanted to move on. How is it that two months after revoking his desire to marry me, he marries her?"

The entire situation piled an enormous load of shame in my heart. I blamed myself for my failing relationship and my backstabbing friends. Something so many of us women do. What did I lack? Did I try hard enough? Was I beautiful? Did I bring anything to the table? Was I wife material? What did another woman have that I did not? These thoughts consumed my mind and caused me to wallow in self-pity. Was I to blame? No. However, that question was a battle for my heart.

I wasn't perfect, but I was sincere in my motives while dating him. Eventually, I realized that it was not my fault, nor the fact that I wasn't good enough. It simply was God's protection! You see, sometimes rejection is protection. It's so hard to understand that concept even as an adult, but it is something that I believe as I look back to the past. I didn't deserve to be mistreated by anyone. God had my best interest at heart and therefore He needed to close the doors of destruction.

Complete healing from my broken heart came a year later and the process of becoming a better woman continued. In addition to a failed romantic relationship, I've experienced the failure of a sibling companionship with my sister (mother's daughter). On occasions I've tried to mend the broken relationship. However, every time I rendered my kindness, she seemed to blame me for life's situations. Accepting the fact that I had to let the idea of having a sister go was a hard pill to swallow. It still is to this day. Accepting this has been the key to forgiveness. Having a female counterpart to chat, shop, and hang out with is something every girl wants. Unfortunately, that's not what I got.

Until my sister allowed God in her heart, we would just be two different people living separate lives. The idea of having a blood sister without having a present connection to her made me feel ashamed. Who's to say that a Christian can get along with everyone, even family? Desiring a connection with my sister and her family was what I longed for, except I was constantly faced with rejection. Knowing that God had my best interest at heart, I continued to pray to God for a sister in Christ who would love me as if we were flesh and blood. I made up in my mind to forgive my sister and loved her at a distance. As life has continued, I've had many other disappointments. Can you relate? Look at your life. What areas are you ashamed of? As you begin to face the shame think about this story. Adam and Eve found in Genesis 2:25-3:20 of the Bible.

When Adam and Eve were created, they were created as naked beings physically, emotionally, and spiritually. They were created with what I call, shameless nakedness. This means that there was openness between both and their creator, God. Their shameless nakedness created an atmosphere of trust, self-worth, true love, and compassion. As you read the story, you will discover that Adam and Eve lost their shameless nakedness when they ate the forbidden fruit. "When the woman saw that the fruit of the tree was good for food and pleasing to the eye, and also desirable for gaining wisdom, she took some and ate it. She also gave some to her husband, who was with her, and he ate it" (Genesis 3:6).

They did not listen to their creator and decided to make a choice against what He wanted for them both. Instead, Adam and Eve followed the voice of a stranger, a serpent, whom led them down a dreary pathway. Genesis 3:1 says, "Now the serpent was craftier than any of the wild animals the LORD God had made. He said to the woman, "Did God really say, 'You must not eat from any tree in the garden?" Following this stranger's advice caused them to lose their shameless nakedness and become clothed in shameful nudity. "He answered, "I heard you in the garden, and I was afraid because I was naked; so I hid" (Genesis 3:10).

After being stripped, a sense of guilt, shame, and vulgar nudity hovered over Adam and Eve. No longer were they shameless. No longer did they feel secure in themselves or with their creator. What happened? Why did they become ashamed of their nakedness? The answer is Sin. Sin is when choices are made opposite to what God desires. It means that we missed the mark, so to speak. When the couple ate the forbidden fruit, they made a bad choice, and missed the mark. Sin entered their lives.

"Then the eyes of both of them were opened, and they realized they were naked; so they sewed fig leaves together and made coverings for themselves" (Genesis 3:7). Sin began to clothe them in shameful nakedness. Realizing that they both were no longer clothed in glory, Adam and Eve decided to cover

18

their shameful nakedness by using fig leaves (Genesis 3:7). The problem was that the leaves would eventually wither and dry. Fig leaves were only temporary. The leaves could not cover their shameful nudity forever, but somehow the two did not realize that. Have you been trying to cover your shame with temporary leaves?

For the same reason shameful nudity entered the lives of Adam and Eve, it enters our lives. Our shame comes as a result of our sins, generational sins, or the sinful things that others have done to us. These sins stamp a tattoo of shame across our hearts. Despite our shameful circumstances, there is a solution to resolve our shame and it's not fig leaves. Our fig leaves can be:

❖ Alcohol
❖ Food
❖ Addictions
❖ Drugs
❖ Relationships
❖ Sex/lust
❖ Money
❖ Popularity/fame
❖ Cars
❖ Houses/property
❖ Brands/labels
❖ Approval from others
❖ Degrees/titles
❖ Medications

These are things that we use to cover our disgrace. God sees you trying to cover your shame. He even knows that your fig leaves are temporary. The leaves will one day wither and dry, leaving you to be shamefully nude. God wants to cover you with His "lasting cloth," like He did for Adam and Eve. He wants to make a sacrifice for you. Genesis 3:21 says, "The LORD God made garments of skin for Adam and his wife and clothed them."

He took away their temporary fig leaves and replaced them with the skin of a sacrificed animal. God sacrificed the life of an innocent animal to cover the shame of Adam and Eve's sin. The ultimate punishment for their disobedience was total annihilation. "In fact, the law requires that nearly everything be cleansed with blood and without the shedding of blood there is no forgiveness" (Hebrews 9:22). Yet God spared their lives by transferring their punishment onto an innocent creature.

Through this sacrifice Adam and Eve's lives, along with their future, were spared. The sacrifice covered their shame forever. This example of a bloody sacrifice of that animal shows us how Jesus would later sacrifice His life to cover our shame. John 3:16-17 reads, "For God so loved the world that he gave his one and only Son, that whoever believes in him shall not perish but have eternal life. For God did not send his Son into the world to condemn the world, but to save the world through him." God wants to wipe away your shame with the garment of Jesus' blood. He wants to turn your old into new. God wants to reverse your past with His future.

~From Shame to Acceptance Challenge~

Today perform a life review to uncover the reason(s) for your shame. Dig deep to figure out what are your temporary fig leaves. Confess these very things to God and ask Him to cover your shame with a lasting sacrifice. Place every shameful thought onto paper and read it aloud. When you finish reading those thoughts trust that God will remove this shame and cover your nakedness with His sacrifice.

~Life Scriptures~

"For God so loved the world that he gave his one and only Son, that whoever believes in him shall not perish but have eternal life. For God did not send his Son into the world to condemn the world, but to save the world through him. Whoever believes in him is not condemned, but whoever does not believe stands condemned already because he has not believed in the name of God's one and only Son" (John 3:16-18).

~Points to Ponder~

❖ What areas of your life have caused you to feel ashamed?
❖ Which fig leaves are you using to temporarily cover your shame?
❖ Have you allowed God to erase your shame with His blood and cover you in His lasting cloth?
❖ Begin a life review today. Journal your experience of moving from feelings of shame to feelings of acceptance in the "My Note Pad" section.

❖ Make a list of things that cause you shame, a list of your fig leaves, and read them out loud. Afterwards stomp on the list, shred, burn, or rip it apart. Reflect on what this exercise signifies.

~Complete a Life Review~

1. Start the review beginning with your childhood.
2. Uncover each traumatic experience that has negatively impacted your life up to this point.
3. Jot these in your note pad.
4. Keep this list in mind as you incorporate these experiences into the additional chapter exercises.

CHAPTER 2

LETTING GO OF PAST PAINS

While walking along the paths of our life we will encounter roadblocks. These roadblocks have the potential to deter us from the finish line. We may encounter a stop sign, roadkill, quicksand, or a pothole. None of us wants to encounter roadblocks because stop signs cause us to become stagnant. Roadkill is stinky. Quicksand swallows us up. Potholes cause damage to our feet and causes us to stumble. The bottom line is that roadblocks stop us from going forward. Roadblocks are culprits in deterring us from reaching our destination.

Not one of these situations brings us any good. I mean how can being stopped or deterred in life help us? Is there any benefit? Can the negative issues we face benefit us? Can heartache, pain, bitterness, resentment, fear, and betrayal, help us in our personal growth? Right now, you are probably thinking that the answer is, "No." Experiencing life's roadblocks causes us to become heavily burdened. My answer to you comes in the form of a question. Can life's issues affect us in a negative way when we do not allow them to do so?

Understand this, only if we allow our issues to consume our mind, body, and spirit, will we crush under the weight of their burden. If we allow the negativity to consume us, then it will crush us. The negativity will leave us tied to its bondage and cause us to slowly lose ourselves to insanity. Not only is our mind and soul affected, but also our physical being. When we become overwhelmed with negative issues, serious health conditions can result. Stress is a co-factor to many diseases. In fact, stress can become so overwhelming that a woman may take her own life. Life's issues are burdensome. Being tangled with them disables us from moving forward. We become disabled emotionally, spiritually, physically, and socially.

How we function in life becomes ineffective. We become women walking around outwardly appearing to be alive, but inwardly dead. We become the living dead because our purpose and meaning for life has been lost. This only happens when we allow our negative issues to consume us. Look around. How many women do you know that say they don't care about life anymore? How many women would rather be dead? How many of us have given up on life? I bet when you begin to count, you will run out of space

22

within your mind. Why do women allow themselves to become entangled in life's issues? The answer is simple. We are human. Women are emotional human beings.

We were designed to love and to be loved. When life throws us the opposite of love (or positive things) we become disheartened. As women, we are emotional and internalize our feelings. It's our innate design to be "internalist". We take every bad external circumstance and make it an internal problem. What am I saying? I am saying that because of your design as a woman, when someone or thing hurts you externally, you meditate on the problem constantly. You allow your heart to embrace the hurt. By embracing the hurt, you begin to identify yourself as the hurt. You define yourself as a hurting woman. Maybe you even call yourself a bitter woman (or a bitch). Have you ever identified yourself as a mad, bitter woman? This is a sign of how we allow ourselves to be identified as our issues. We allow bad circumstances to define our worth.

There are examples of this everywhere. Women are holding onto their past hurts, downfalls, issues, and current problems. Women are giving signs that they are still hurting, not over their problems, angry, and stagnant in moving forward in their life. What is the excuse? "I am human and its human nature to hold onto my issues, grudges, and leave my issues unsolved." Sadly, we excuse ourselves to hold onto the negative circumstances that chain us to our roadblocks. During my years of living, I've learned that the hardest thing for us to do is move forward with our life.

Humans can create the most magnificent buildings, air crafts, and paintings, but we find it hard to move forward. In moving forward, we must forgive ourselves and others for past circumstances. That's what makes it so difficult to let go of the negativity. Apostle Paul said, "Be kind and compassionate to one another, forgiving each other, just as in Christ forgave you" (Ephesians 4:32). In this passage, Paul instructs us to forgive everyone, even our enemies. He instructs us to forgive others just as God has forgiven us. We forget how many times God forgave us.

Haven't we hurt God? Haven't we wrongly accused or done things to other people? Why do we forget that we too have messed up? We need forgiveness and countless times God forgave us. So why is it that when other people do us wrong, we don't want to forgive them? Doesn't this sound hypocritical? We ask to be forgiven, but we cannot administer forgiveness. Does it do us good to hold anger and resentment in our hearts? Do we think about the toil it takes on our spiritual, emotional, mental, and physical health?

Un-forgiveness is destructive. It causes you to become hateful, bitter, resentful, shameful, and stagnant on your pathway. Un-forgiveness is the most powerful roadblock of all. Jesus Christ tells us in Matthew 6:14-15, "For if you forgive other people when they sin against you, your heavenly Father will also forgive you. But if you do not forgive others their sins, your Father will not forgive your sins." God is letting us know that it would be hypocritical for us to ask for His forgiveness and turn around to not forgive others. We are called to be like Christ. Therefore, we must begin to forgive other people despite what they did to bring harm. We must forgive them and ourselves to remove the roadblocks. Forgiveness is a process that opens our hearts to forgive others and embrace God's forgiveness for ourselves.

~Process of Forgiveness~

1) Remove the belief that you have the right to get even with people who hurt you.
2) Re-examine your life. Look at the past circumstances and analyze the details.
3) What are possible reasons for the person's actions or remarks? Were they treated the same way in their past? Are they repeating a cycle? Do they realize that what they did negatively affected you? Try to see the bigger picture.
4) Embrace the belief that forgiveness heals you, not necessarily your forgiver. Forgiveness is for you. It breaks you free from feelings of resentment, hatred, bondage, and grief. Forgiveness removes the roadblocks of your life.

~Letting Go of Past Pains Challenge~

Today, I challenge you to begin your journey to forgiveness! Ask God to reveal to you everyone you need forgive. Meditate about your life and remember those people you have not forgiven. It's not worth it to hold a grudge against anyone. In the long run you're hurting yourself. Un-forgiveness creates a heart full of heavy chains, resentment, shame, and sadness. The person you hate is living their life while you are stuck in the muck of your bitterness. They are not worried about you. They have moved on, but you have not.

Let God take away your chains of hatred and bitterness through the process of forgiveness. Allow joy and peace to encompass you. Begin to live a life of freedom starting today. Warning: the process of forgiveness is not easy. It's painful, but it ends in joy. Helpful tip: Do not focus on the pain. Focus on the purpose.

~Life Scriptures~

"Then Peter came to Jesus and asked, "Lord, how many times shall I forgive my brother or sister who sins against me? Up to seven times?" Jesus answered, "I tell you, not seven times, but seventy-seven times." Therefore, the kingdom of heaven is like a king who wanted to settle accounts with his servants. As he began the settlement, a man who owed him ten thousand bags of gold was brought to him. Since he was not able to pay, the master ordered that he and his wife and his children and all that he had be sold to repay the debt. At this the servant fell on his knees before him. "Be patient with me," he begged, "and I will pay back everything." The servant's master took pity on him, canceled the debt and let him go. But when that servant went out, he found one of his fellow servants who owed him a hundred silver coins (denarii). He grabbed him and began to choke him. "Pay back what you owe me!" He demanded. His fellow servant fell to his knees and begged him, "Be patient with me, and I will pay you back." But he refused. Instead, he went off and had the man thrown into prison until he could pay the debt. When the other servants saw what had happened, they were outraged and went and told their master everything that had happened. Then the master called the servant in. "You wicked servant," he said, "I canceled all that debt of yours because you begged me to. Shouldn't you have had mercy on your fellow servant just as I had on you?" In anger his master turned him over to the jailers to be tortured, until he should pay back all he owed. This is how my heavenly Father will treat each of you unless you forgive your brother from your heart" (Matthew 18:21-35).

"And when you stand praying, if you hold anything against anyone, forgive him, so that your Father in heaven may forgive you your sins" (Mark 11:25).

"Bear with each other and forgive whatever grievances you may have against one another. Forgive as the Lord forgave you" (Colossians 3:13).

~Points to Ponder~

❖ What is forgiveness?

❖ Why is forgiveness important?

❖ Who or what do you need to forgive?

❖ Is there anyone you need to ask to forgive you?

❖ Have you accepted God's forgiveness?

Below is a prose that I wrote at a moment in my life when I needed to forgive people who deeply hurt me. I knew that in order to heal and move forward with my life, I had to forgive them. No matter how hard it would be, I had to let it go. I pray this prose changes your life as much as it changed mine!

LET IT GO

God?

Yes my child, what is it?

Are you still there?

Yes my child, I'm still here and I always will be.

Really?

Yes really, why would I ever leave you?

Because.

Because what?

Me!

You?

Yes me, I'm messed up!

Do you think that I didn't know? (God chuckles)

I know you said you'll love me in spite of my mess, but I've truly messed up this time around!

My child you're acting as though you don't mess up DAILY!

Do I?

Yes my child, you do. However, let's get back to what you were going to tell me.

Well, first God, I want to say thank you for saving me and delivering me daily!

My child, no problem! I love you too much not to.

Thank you and I don't deserve that kind of love.

Heavenly Father, it hurts. What I'm going through hurts.

LET IT GO.

But Lord, I feel like I want to just die.

LET IT GO.

But Lord, they left me.

LET IT GO.

But Lord, I'm selfish.

LET IT GO.

But Lord, we've been together for so long.

LET IT GO.

But Lord, the Crystal Methamphetamine (drugs) takes away the pain.

LET IT GO.

But Lord, it feels good to please myself.

LET IT GO.

But Lord, I don't feel like letting it go.

LET IT GO.

But Lord, she did me so wrong.

LET IT GO.

But Lord, he did me so wrong.

LET IT GO.

But Lord, the situation is overwhelming.

LET IT GO.

But God, the alcohol takes the pain away.

LET IT GO.

But Lord, cutting my body is a display of my pain.

MY CHILD, NO. LET IT GO!

But Lord, he never pays child support.

LET IT GO.

But Lord, going to the club satisfies my soul.

LET IT GO.

But Lord, he's never there.

LET IT GO.

I have too much baggage.

LET IT GO.

But Lord, what about the memories?

LET IT GO.

But Lord, they're dead and I'll never touch them again.

LET IT GO.

But Lord, I long for his touch.

LET IT GO.

But Lord, I hate my facial features.

LET IT GO.

But Lord, I feel unworthy.

LET IT GO.

But Lord, I feel hatred toward myself.

LET IT GO.

But Lord, I fear achieving my goals.

LET IT GO.

But Lord, my dad was never there.

LET IT GO.

But Lord, my career seems impossible to achieve.

LET IT GO.

But Lord, my mother never truly cared.

LET IT GO.

But Lord, sex feels so good.

LET IT GO.

But Lord, home girl is so fine.

LET IT GO.

But Lord, they hate my guts and we're family.

LET IT GO.

But Lord, we were so close.

LET IT GO.

But Lord, he was my husband, my man.

LET IT GO.

But Lord, he abused me.

LET IT GO.

But Lord, I feel like I'll never be a good man.

LET IT GO.

But Lord, I hate the system.

LET IT GO.

But Lord, the devil gave me these chains.

LET IT GO.

But Lord, I made too many mistakes.

LET IT GO.

But Lord, church folks hate me.

LET IT GO.

But Lord, I turned from you.

I KNOW! I LET IT GO!

But Lord, I hated you.

I KNOW! I LET IT GO!

But Lord, I did you so wrong.

I KNOW! I LET IT GO!

But Lord, they did you wrong.

I KNOW! I LET IT GO!

But Lord, I am not like you!

How am I supposed to let it go?

How am I supposed to let it all go?

MY CHILD, YOU HAVE TO GIVE IT TO ME!

In order to let go of your issues you must give them to God.

Chapter 3

It was Necessary

Have you asked yourself this question; why did this happen to me? Maybe you want to know why you encountered certain situations? Things like abuse, frustration, un-planned pregnancy, loss of a job, or discrimination. Based on chapter 2, now you understand that you must let the past go, but what was the purpose of all the negativity? Why did he/she hurt you? Why should you forgive them? Why did you make bad choices? Should you forgive yourself? Why did God allow these situations to happen? Millions of women ask these exact questions.

All of us have encountered circumstances that took away our happiness. Each time a negative circumstance enters our life our hopes die. I don't know what obstacles you have endured. Maybe your life has been so bad that you'd rather not live. What I do know is that God has given you the ability to endure through the negativity because you're still alive. Maybe you're thinking, "Yes, I've endured the trials and I'm physically alive, but my circumstances have emotionally killed me."

To be killed means to cease, no longer exist. It is the opposite of life. So, to be emotionally killed means to be emotionally non-existent. It means to be an emotionally dead woman. Death isn't limited to the physical, it comes in different forms. Death can be emotional, spiritual, and/or mental. I have discovered that emotional death is the worse. Emotional death leaves us physically alive while we rot inside. The core of our being dies. When we are emotionally dead, we walk around deceiving others with a facade that we are alive, but if other people knew the truth, they'd find that we are dying from the inside out. You can't feel anything. Nothing matters anymore. Your body was once full of vitality and is now lifeless.

Maybe you've tried everything to revive your soul. Possibly you've tried to go to church, but it didn't work. Maybe you tried to find a new romance, but you remain un-revived. You've tried embracing the love of others, but it's not enough. Alcohol, drugs, money, and sex; you've tried them all. Sadly, you remain unable to be emotionally revitalized. Your soul is screaming for restoration! Your heart needs to be revived, but where can you find healing if it can't be found anywhere you've looked?

I am writing to let you know that church, a new romance, or material things cannot bring healing. These things don't have enough of an electrical shock to revive your heart. What you need to do is connect with a supernatural power. This is a power source that can pierce through your body tissue and into your soul. Only supernatural power can heal the soul. The things of our natural realm can never provide us with what is needed supernaturally. You can't take an Aspirin or Motrin to make emotional pain go away. You can take this for a physical wound, but not an emotional wound.

A physical wound can also be healed with bandages, antibiotics, and pain medicine. You can rub hydrogen peroxide on the wound and suture it with bandages. However, when our hearts receive cuts from life's blows, none of these medications, bandages, antibiotics, and/or sutures can fix the problem. So, if God knew there was not any natural healing for our wounded hearts, why did He allow hurtful things to happen? How can we heal?

My sister that's what I am here to tell you. There is no form of healing for your heart here on Earth. There are not any special bandages big enough to fit your wounds. There are no medications strong enough to get rid of your emotional pain. However, there is a supernatural force dwelling in our infinite universe. This force can supernaturally cut through your skin, reach your heart, and heal the wounds (pain). What is this force? This force is your divine creator, God. God has the power to heal your broken heart and revitalize your soul. John 11:25 says, "I am the resurrection and the life. He who believes in me, will live, even though he dies."

Let's put this in the context of emotional pain. Jesus is saying, although you are severely wounded and emotionally dead, He has the power to revitalize your heart. How awesome is that? During times in my life (many times) my heart is wounded. I feel internally rotten. This Scripture is a constant reminder that God can give me the ability to live again. I can account that what Jesus says in John 11:25 is true. Not only can God revive your heart, He can answer the question as to why hurtful things happen to you.

His answer may be that it was for your personal growth. The answer may be that He wanted you to understand His supernatural power. Sometimes we don't recognize the power of God until we've exhausted every other failed attempt to heal ourselves. A personal example is, when I am deeply hurting, God strips people and things from my life. It is not an easy thing to accept. Although my family or friends can give me advice on how to heal, my heart remains wounded. Church sermons don't work. Friendly comfort does not either. I still hurt.

All these things assist in my healing, but they do not bring my healing to completion. Nothing works until I embrace the divine love of God. God is the only thing that seems to love me past my pain. He can heal my wounded soul. During the painful times I ask God why He allows hurtful things to happen to me? The answer I receive seems to always be that it's necessary. "And we know that in all things God works for the good of those who love him, who have been called according to his purpose" (Romans 8:28). God tells me that the purpose of my emotional pain is for personal growth. He wants me to understand His ability to supernaturally revive my heart. He wants me to understand who He and His desire is to love me.

Most of all, He wanted to use my hurts as life lessons. You're probably wondering what the purpose of your pain is. God will give you the answer as you ask and complete a life reflection. His answer may not come with extravagant detail. God's answers are sometimes simple. No matter how simple or extravagant the answer is, you will find one underlying factor, each situation we go through in life serves as a necessity for our personal growth.

~It was Necessary Challenge~

Here is the challenge, understand that every situation in your life serves a specific purpose. Its purpose may be extravagantly important or simple, but it's necessary. Below is a poem that I wrote when I questioned God why my life seemed to be failing. I pray that after reading the poem you will grasp why God allowed hurtful things to happen to you too. Expect God to heal your wounded heart and revive your dying soul.

~Life Scriptures~

"On his arrival, Jesus found that Lazarus had already been in the tomb for four days. Bethany was less than two miles from Jerusalem, and many Jews had come to Martha and Mary to comfort them in the loss of their brother. When Martha heard that Jesus was coming, she went out to meet him, but Mary stayed at home. "Lord," Martha said to Jesus, "if you had been here, my brother would not have died. But I know that even now God will give you whatever you ask." Jesus said to her, "Your brother will rise again." Martha answered, "I know he will rise again in the resurrection at the last day." Jesus said to her, "I am the resurrection and the life. He who believes in me will live, even though he dies; and whoever lives and believes in me will never die. Do you believe this?" (John 11:17-26).

"And we know that in all things God works for the good of those who love him, who have been called according to his purpose" (Romans 8:28).

~Points to Ponder~

❖ What has caused your emotional pain?

❖ What ways are you trying to heal your broken heart?

❖ Have these worked? Why or why not?

❖ Will you give God a chance to heal your wounded heart and revitalize your life?

❖ Discuss within a group the common ways that women try to heal from their pain.

❖ Which ways seem to be the most effective?

❖ Within your group allow each person to speak an encouraging word to each other.

❖ After reading the poem below. Create your own.

IT WAS NECESSARY

Your lies
were necessary.
Your infidelity
was necessary.
Your dirty comments
were necessary.
Your hate
was necessary.
Your fakeness
was necessary.
You copping out on love
was necessary.
Your backstabbing
was necessary.
Trying to emotionally control me
was necessary.
The loss of your friendship
was necessary.
The tears I cried
were necessary.
My bitterness
was necessary.
My anxiety
was necessary.
My lack of comfort
was necessary.
My weakness
was necessary.
My stupidity
was necessary.
My disobedience
was necessary.
Your laughter
was necessary.
The death of your love towards me
was necessary.

34

How could this be?
Your lies
made me trust God.
Your infidelity
showed me your character.
Your dirty comments
pushed me to God's throne.
Your hate
taught me to love myself.
Your fakeness
showed me how real is God.
You copping out on love
showed me how weak you were.
Your backstabbing
showed me who was on my side.
Your emotional control
showed me how strong I was.
The loss of our friendship
showed me we were never intimate.
The tears I cried
made me vulnerable to God and stronger in the process.
My bitterness
drove me to change my attitude.
My anxiety
placed a feeling inside, to let you go.
After that, it taught me to trust God and let it go!
My uneasiness
gave me the desire to wait for something better.
My weakness
showed me that only God is strong.
My stupidity
showed me that only God is wise.
My disobedience
always showed me to listen to God.
Your laughter
taught me to pay attention to GOD.
The death of your love towards me allowed me to emotionally die with you
and be revitalized with Christ.

CHAPTER 4

YOU CAN NEVER FAIL

At this point of our journey hopefully you understand that the obstacles you have encountered were necessary for your growth and that you need to let go of the past. However, you may feel like a failure. How can you begin to take the next steps when you feel like a failure? The battles of your life are over, but the war continues. Feelings of being knocked down, pushed around, forsaken, and defeated constantly entertain your mind. I know exactly how you're feeling. You think that your life has reached its end. You feel like you've lost everything. The only cure seems to be to isolate yourself from your dreams, loved ones, and God. You want to accept the idea of being a failure.

You understand that your obstacles were allowed in your life to make you grow into a better woman. Yet, you can't rebound from them. They were failed circumstances in your life. When you think about them, they bring feelings of defeat. You made a vow to, as Jay-Z says, "brush your shoulders off". You want to continue with your life, but it's requiring too much energy. Your life looks tore up from the floor up. The obstacles of your past have robbed you of your future. They have tinted your outlook on life. Life to you now is like a track field which is set to trip you up as you run the course.

I want to tell you today that life is a track field. The key to winning the race is to understand that God is the track. He orchestrates the pathways of your life. He allows you to run into the hurdles of life that will make you stronger, not to trip you. If God wants you to learn a lesson about love and forgiveness, He will allow you to run into heartbreak. If He wants you to experience financial triumph, He will allow you to run into financial burdens. If God believes you need to learn how to trust Him, He will allow you to run into betrayal.

Whichever lessons you need to learn, God will allow you to run into them along your pathway. Life's lessons must be experienced, they cannot be spoon-fed. They must be learned. The way we were designed to learn is through experience and lessons. Your failures are teachers of life's lessons. Without failure, you can't learn. Think about a child who goes in the kitchen and plays next to a hot stove. You tell the child to move away because the stove is hot, and they will get burnt. The child refuses to move and ends up getting burnt. You run to the child and help them cope with the disaster. The next time you tell the child to move away from the stove, they listen because they have learned the effects of encountering a hot stove.

The child never forgets what happened and always stays away from hot stoves. The child failed to listen, but now has learned an important life lesson. Don't touch hot stoves because they will burn you. You see, failures are life's lessons. Sometimes life doesn't go the way we've planned because our plan wasn't the best. Maybe we wanted to touch the hot stove, but God said no! When God is leading our lives, He knows what is best for us. Sometimes God will stop our plans from working in order to protect us. We may view our failed plans as life's failures, but they were plans stopped by God. He didn't want your plans to work out. He knew it wasn't the best thing for you. When something isn't in God's plan, it will not happen.

No matter if you didn't get the position, was laid off, abandoned by lovers, rejected, or lost opportunities, you must remember that what you wanted may not have been in God's plan. No matter what you try to do to make your plans work; they will not happen the way you intend. Your plans will only work the way they have been orchestrated by God. In other words, your life cannot fail! It may seem like failure to you because your mind is too finite to understand God's infinite plans. Your life is a failure according to your mind, but not according to God's.

The failure of your plan is the beginning of God's purpose. Don't look at your past discrepancies as failures; look at them as instances where divine intervention took place. By God stopping your plans, He may have stopped you from taking a job that you would end up hating, marrying someone that would abuse you, or stopped you from making the biggest mistake of your life. When God stops your plans to interject His own, there is a reason. It's not to cause you to fail, but to give you the best. God's plans for your life will never fail. Only our plans fail and when they do, God is there to turn our plans into His own. In other words, He turns our failures into success.

~You Can Never Fail Challenge~

Today, I challenge you to become an ex-failure. Live your life according to God's plan. Allow God the opportunity to guide your life. He wants to orchestrate your pathway of life. Often, we get in the way of God's plan. We try our best to carry out our own plans and they fail. God knows what the best plans for our lives are. He knows how to protect us from failure and destruction. Take today's challenge to erase your plans as God writes His onto your track field.

"David also said to Solomon his son, 'Be strong and courageous, and do the work. Do not be afraid or discouraged, for the Lord God, my God, is with you. He will not fail you or forsake you until all the work for the service of the temple of the Lord is finished" (1 Chronicles 28:20).

"I will maintain my love to him forever, and my covenant with him will never fail. I will establish his line forever, his throne as long as the heavens endure" (Psalm 89:28-29).

"Plans fail for lack of counsel, but with many advisers they succeed" (Proverbs 15:22).

"Has his unfailing love vanished forever? Has his promise failed for all time? Has God forgotten to be merciful? Has he in anger withheld his compassion? Then I thought, 'To this I will appeal: the years of the right hand of the Most High.' I will remember your miracles of long ago. I will meditate on all your works and consider all your mighty deeds" (Psalm 77:8-12).

"He said to me: 'It is done. I am the Alpha and the Omega, the Beginning and the End. To him who is thirsty I will give to drink without cost from the spring of the water of life" (Revelation 21:6).

~Points to Ponder~

❖ Compare and contrast the definitions of failure and success.
❖ Which scriptures indicate that God guides our lives?
❖ Have you made plans that failed? Why did they fail? How do you think God wanted these plans to be carried out?
❖ Have you tried God's plan for your life?
❖ Look at John 1:46. How does this text relate to the concept of failure?
❖ Which scriptures support the idea that God wants you to prosper?
❖ In your note pad write the steps you will take to become an ex-failure.

CHAPTER 5

HOLD ON AND STEP ASIDE

When we struggle, it means that we fight with an opposing force or forces. Opposition can come from people or in the form of negative circumstances. In a spiritual sense, opposition can arise from the dark pits of the supernatural realm. All types of oppositional forces have the power to block us on the road to our destiny. Have you sensed that an unseen force was preventing you from achieving your goals? Did you know who or where these opposing forces were from, but didn't know how to conquer their power? The strength of the force seemed too enormous for you to fight. Therefore, you decided to give up on reaching your destiny. You decide to give up on life and doubt your hope.

While enduring the journey of life, seen and unseen, negative forces will try to overpower you. It is important that you do not lose faith during these times. You must hold onto faith. What is faith? "Now faith is confidence in what we hope for and assurance about what we do not see" (Hebrews 11:1). Faith is an undying sense of hope deep within a person's mind. It is when you believe in something that you can't fathom. Faith believes that you will be alive tomorrow when you wake up. It believes that when everything is going wrong in your life, it will somehow get better. When negative forces come against us in life, we must believe that God is powerful enough to cause us to defeat the opposition. Many times, through bad situations, our sense of hope dies, and we believe in the impossible.

The good thing about opposition is that it can cause us to develop hope in the capabilities of supernatural power. When we realize that something bigger than us is needed in our life, we develop a belief in the supernatural. We develop a faith in God. We realize that He can solve our problems, conquer our battles, and change our circumstances. Through our struggles, we develop a better understanding of God's power. His power ensures us that we are protected when we face opposition. "If the God of my father, the God of Abraham and the fear of Isaac, had not been with me, you surely would have sent me away empty-handed. But God has seen my hardship and the toil of my hands, and last night he rebuked you" (Genesis 31:42).

When questions such as, can God handle my situations? Does He hear me when I call? Is God real? When will my struggles end"; come into your mind, remember His words! There are over 1 million words spoken to you from God. Some of those words are, "I will fight your battles" (2 Chronicles 20:15). The encouragement you need is found in His word, the Bible. Pointers on how to overcome your obstacles are in His word. Every answer can be found in His word. As you deal with opposition, continue developing your faith, and understanding of God's power to conquer your obstacles. "Finally, be strong in the Lord and in his mighty power. Put on the full armor of God so that you can take a stand against the devil's schemes. For our struggle is not against flesh and blood, but against the rulers, against the authorities, against the powers of this dark world and against the spiritual forces of evil in the heavenly realms. Therefore, put on the full armor of God, so that when the day of evil comes, you may be able to stand your ground, and after you have done everything, to stand" (Ephesians 6:10-13).

You must take a stand on faith and trust that God will allow you to hold on until His solution arrives! Over the past few years, I have encountered numerous people who have shared with me their struggles (opposition). There has been so much going wrong within our lives. Starting with the destruction of our global economy, to that of our personal lives, all hell has broken loose. Many of us over the years have found ourselves robbed of our destiny. We have been assaulted emotionally, physically, financially, and in every other way. As a result, many of us have or are losing our faith in a higher power.

Life's issues are weighing down on our hearts and minds. I can bet that during the past few years, you too have encountered opposition. Maybe your life is beyond crazy right now, but keep in mind that you're not alone. The journey of life is full of opposition, struggles, obstacles, mishaps, and setbacks. However, while the children of God are struggling, we must recognize that we don't have to fight our battles. 2 Chronicles 20:15 reads, "He said: 'Listen, King Jehoshaphat and all who live in Judah and Jerusalem! This is what the Lord says to you:' 'Do not be afraid or discouraged because of this vast army. For the battle is not yours, but God's.'"

This scripture informs us that during times of opposition we should not be afraid or discouraged. We must hold on and step aside. The road of life can get rocky, your pathway may get cloudy, your walk may become a limp, and your hope may dwindle, but hold on to your faith. Continue to trust God. Believe that He will not give you a challenge that you and He cannot conquer. You must continue to hold on to hope because there are other people that need to see you conquer life's opposing forces. They need to hear your story. There are others that need to see how God pulled you out of your deepest despair. God desires to use your opposition to reveal His power.

He equips us with His strength to endure and conquer our trials. "No temptation has seized you except what is common to man. And God is faithful; he will not let you be tempted beyond what you can bear. But when you are tempted, he will also provide a way out so that you can stand up under it" (1 Corinthians 10:13). God can defeat your opposing forces. He can get you out of your bad circumstances. The key is to hold on to your faith.

~Hold on and Step Aside Challenge~

My challenge to you is to read the entire chapter of Hebrews 11. This chapter is filled with inspiration and provides wisdom about faith. While reading Hebrews 11, take time to reflect on how you can incorporate faith into your life. Reflect over your obstacles and losses. How did faith play or not play a role in each circumstance? Today, choose to make a difference in your life by developing faith in God. He can make the impossible, possible. He can make the weary, strong. God can make the blind see. He can make your pathway purposeful. Decide to believe that God's power can defeat your opposition. You have tried everything else. Why not try faith?

~Life Scriptures~

Hebrews 11:1-3 reads, "Now faith is being sure of what we hope for and certain of what we do not see. This is what the ancients were commended for. By faith we understand that the universe was formed at God's command, so that what was seen was not made out of what was visible."

"When people do not accept divine guidance, they run wild. But whoever obeys the law is joyful" (Proverbs 29:18, NLT).

~Points to Ponder~

❖ What opposition have you faced, or are you currently facing?
❖ What have you built your faith on? Has it been money, careers, friends, or God?
❖ Has your faith worked in solving your problems? Why or why not?
❖ Define faith in your own words and find supporting scriptures.
❖ Define trust in your own words. How does this definition go along with

faith?

❖ How can the concept of "holding on" change your negative circumstances?

Chapter 6

As God Speaks

God speaks,

Come here my lover.
Come here and have a cup of tea.
Sit here at my table.
Come here and sit with me.

How have you been?
What have you been up to?
Has anyone told you how much I love you?

I knew you before you were born.
I knew all the tears you would cry when you felt alone.

So, come here. Come with me.
I promise I can tell all your tears to be gone.

When I speak this into existence they will go away.
Why don't you come here lover?
Come and sit beside me.

What have you been up to?
Where have you been?
I have been sitting here, right here, with this cup of tea.

The tea is now cold because you took so long.
Please come here. There is no time to prolong.

Don't prolong my waiting time to speak to you.
Why don't you love the One who died just for you?

I can tell you your future.
I can see it all the way to the end.
I can even tell you how time began.

First, you must come and sit with me.

Why such sorrow?
Why such pain?
Why can't you stand the rain?

Tell me, ask me, and I will answer every plea.
From sorrow, sickness, and burdens, I can set you free.

Did you know that I own the universe?
I can take away all your hurt.

I am your God!
Did you not know?

Did you think I died on the cross for a talent show?
I died to show you how much I care.

So please, come and sit here.
Sit here beside me. Listen to all that I have to say.
Talk to me lover. Talk to me throughout your day.

When you come, I will say, thank you for coming to me.
Let's bargain together.
Let me set you free.

Free from your sorrow.
Free from pain.
Not to mention, I can shelter you from the rain.

What is GOD trying to speak to your heart today?

~As God Speaks Challenge~

Your challenge today is to place God in the highest priority of your life. It's a tough challenge for most of us. We usually make our beauty, finances, and especially men, our priority. This is because we live in a society were materialistic things is thought to satisfy our hearts. As women, especially Christians, we should realize that nothing in this world can bring true joy or everlasting satisfaction. We were not made to receive eternal joy from material things. That is why we constantly search for something better.

The material things in our world should not be our top priority. Instead the One, whose hands were pierced, should be. I challenge you to place the Almighty Creator in first place of your life. Don't place Him on the back burner where He is waiting to have a "cup of tea" with you. Otherwise, you will not find out what He has to say to you and miss your destiny!

~Life Scriptures~

"But seek first his kingdom and his righteousness, and all these things will be given to you as well" (Mathew 6:33).

"Do not conform any longer to the pattern of this world, but be transformed by the renewing of your mind. Then you will be able to test and approve what God's will is-his good, pleasing and perfect will" (Romans 12:2).

~Points to Ponder~

❖ How is your spiritual relationship with the creator?

❖ When was the last time you had a heart-to-heart conversation with God?

❖ What is your top priority? How does this priority serve a purpose in your life?

❖ How do material things satisfy you? What supports this viewpoint? Is it true?

❖ What should be your top priority?

❖ Which things satisfy human hearts?

CHAPTER 7

MOVE QUICKLY

I remember in 2007 during the last week of November a gloomy and weird feeling came upon me. I could not figure out why this feeling came. It was like a dark cloud came out from nowhere and decided to hang itself over my head. Months prior to November I had experienced what I thought was the worse time of my life. Since then, I've experienced more difficulty. I was hurt by the person I loved. I lost a few friends. God was stripping people and things from my life. This caused pain. God was moving quickly in my life. He took me out of a failing relationship, friendships, and life circumstances. Perhaps God wants to take you out of similar situations. Looking at my life now, I understand the reason why God did those things. He was saving me from making decisions I would regret.

During that week November 2007, I did a lot of introspection. I reflected on my life's journey. I reflected over my hurts. At that point of time, I didn't believe I would heal from the hurt. People tried to encourage me, but the pain never subsided. Even though I smiled, I was hurting. It took some time, but eventually the pain disappeared. I was able to smile from the inside out. If you are experiencing pain and it seems like you'll never heal, I want to reassure you that your healing will arrive one day.

One day you'll reflect over your life and realize that the pain disappeared. You will realize that you made it through the toughest time of your life. Healing will come to your door and the pain will disappear. I will not tell you that your healing will happen fast. Neither will I say that it will take a long time. I will say this, with the right amount of time, your healing will arrive. God works in the best timing for each of us. He knows how much time we need to deal with and heal from our issues. Depending on the issue the healing process can be short, or very long. No matter how long or short the process is, we must remember that God does what is best for us. "Being confident of this, that he who began a good work in you will carry it on to completion until the day of Christ Jesus" (Philippians 1:6).

God cares about every adversity we face. He cares about every tear. He wants to heal your hurt. God is saying to you, "I am here for you. Let Me take you through the healing process. Get back up, dust the dirt off your shoulders, and stop thinking you will never heal. Don't worry about when your healing will arrive, just know that it will happen." It is time to decide whether you want God to make a move in your life. It may not be at the time you want. It will be on God's timing. The best timing of all.

~Move Quickly Challenge~

My challenge to you is to allow God to make a move in your life according to His timing, not your own. When we make moves according to our timing, we end up doing things off schedule. Often, we do things out of order. Think about when you tried to fix a problem according to your timing. How did it work?

For example, have you forced a friendship to happen because you were lonely? That same relationship probably turned sour and made you realize that it failed because it was the wrong time. You should have let the relationship grow in its own timing, but you forced it.

We force a lot of things in our lives. We constantly force things to happen at the wrong time, instead of letting them happen on God's timing. Starting today take a chill pill. Let God set your schedule. Move quickly out of God's way so that He can make a move in your life.

~Life Scriptures~

"He said to them: "It is not for you to know the times or dates the Father has set by his own authority"" (Acts 1:7).

"Not that I have already obtained all this, or have already arrived at my goal, but I press on to take hold of that for which Christ Jesus took hold of me. Brothers and sisters, I do not consider myself yet to have taken hold of it. But one thing I do: Forgetting what is behind and straining toward what is ahead, I press on toward the goal to win the prize for which God has called me heavenward in Christ Jesus" (Philippians 3: 12-14).

"But forget all that- it is nothing compared to what I am going to do. For I am about to do something new. See, I have already begun! Do you not see it?" (Isaiah 43:18-19, NLT).

"The righteous keep moving forward and those with clean hands become stronger and stronger" (Job 17:9).

"He said: 'Listen, King Jehoshaphat and all who live in Judah and Jerusalem! This is what the Lord says to you: 'Do not be afraid or discouraged because of this vast army. For the battle is not yours, but God's" (2 Chronicles 20:15).

~Points to Ponder~

- ❖ How have you hindered God from making a move in your life?
- ❖ What do you want to change about your life?
- ❖ In your own terms define the words hindrance, mistrust, disobedience, faith, trust, and hope.
- ❖ How are these words relevant to what we've talked about in this chapter? Give supporting scriptures.
- ❖ Journal in your note pad a situation where you forced something to happen in your life. What were the results.
- ❖ What can you learn from this situation?
- ❖ Why is it important to do things according to God's schedule?

CHAPTER 8

THOUGH HE SLAY ME

Each of us has a God-given pathway that we must travel in order to reach our destination which is ultimately heaven. As we journey along our pathway, there will be times when the road is smooth and easy. There will also be times when the journey is rough and rugged. Potholes, rocks, and puddles will find their way onto our path, stopping us from reaching our destination. These roadblocks become hindrances to our strength, faith, and commitment to the destination. They cause us to question if we want to continue the path. Examples of roadblocks are:

- ❖ Financial hardship
- ❖ Social persecution
- ❖ Abandonment
- ❖ Discrimination
- ❖ Illness
- ❖ Change
- ❖ Age
- ❖ Unhealthy relationships
- ❖ Death or a loss

At some point these will appear on your path. I personally like to think of roadblocks as "testers." These are things that test our faith and commitment to following God's pathway. When our pathway is smooth, we often do not question our commitment. It is when the terrain becomes rugged, we want to choose a different pathway. We'd much rather a pathway without any hassle, struggle, or problems. However, even with faith in God, bad things will happen. Even when we choose to remain committed to the pathway, we will meet roadblocks. Life is not hassle free.

You will be ridiculed, people will hurt you, and unpleasant things will happen. No matter how committed you are to God and following your pathway, you will not escape problems. Sometimes when multiple problems arise it seems as though God himself made the pathway rugged. During times like these we are slain. Slain is a state of being put to death. Let's look at a biblical story where God's faithful servant felt this way. Let's examine his pathway, how he reacted to the roadblocks, and what was the outcome. Before proceeding, please read the entire book of Job. After reading this story you will notice that Job's pathway was smooth in the beginning. He was financially, socially, and spiritually successful. Job had faith in God and was committed to his pathway. He had a wife, successful children, riches, and a strong communion with God. Job had everything he wanted.

However, one day multiple roadblocks entered his pathway and everything he had was destroyed. The calamity that happened was not just happenstance, it was planned. These roadblocks were designed to destroy his faith and commitment to follow his God-given pathway. We read that God allowed this to happen because He knew Job would still serve Him despite the roadblocks he faced. "One day the angels came to present themselves before the LORD, and Satan also came with them. The LORD said to Satan, "Where have you come from?" Satan answered the LORD, "From roaming throughout the earth, going back and forth on it." Then the LORD said to Satan, "Have you considered my servant Job? There is no one on earth like him; he is blameless and upright, a man who fears God and shuns evil." "Does Job fear God for nothing?" Satan replied. "Have you not put a hedge around him and his household and everything he has? You have blessed the work of his hands, so that his flocks and herds are spread throughout the land. But now stretch out your hand and strike everything he has, and he will surely curse you to your face." The LORD said to Satan, "Very well, then, everything he has is in your power, but on the man himself do not lay a finger." Then Satan went out from the presence of the LORD" (Job 1:6-12).

An important question that we must ask ourselves, like Job, is "will I follow God when roadblocks enter my pathway and cause calamity in my life?" "One day when Job's sons and daughters were feasting and drinking wine at the oldest brother's house, a messenger came to Job and said, "The oxen were plowing and the donkeys were grazing nearby, and the Sabeans attacked and made off with them. They put the servants to the sword, and I am the only one who has escaped to tell you!" While he was still speaking, another messenger came and said, "The fire of God fell from the heavens and burned up the sheep and the servants, and I am the only one who has escaped to tell you!"

"While he was still speaking, another messenger came and said, "The Chaldeans formed three raiding parties and swept down on your camels and made off with them. They put the servants to the sword, and I am the only one who has escaped to tell you!" While he was still speaking, yet another messenger came and said, "Your sons and daughters were feasting and drinking wine at the oldest brother's house, when suddenly a mighty wind swept in from the desert and struck the four corners of the house. It collapsed on them and they are dead, and I am the only one who has escaped to tell you!" At this, Job got up and tore his robe and shaved his head. Then he fell to the ground in worship" (Job 1:13-20).

Job had his wealth, family, wife, friend's trust, and health. The calamity destroyed everything. However, Job remained faithful in trusting God. He remained committed to walking the pathway to his destination. Job believed that even if God brought the calamity into his life everything would get better. "Though he slay me, yet will I hope in him; I will surely defend my ways to his face" (Job 13:15). Job was a committed man of God. However, his life was not exempt from problems. Job faced persecution, rejection, betrayal, loneliness, sickness, financial hardships, loss of family, loss of friendships, and false accusation from those whom he loved.

The amazing thing about Job's situation, which may depict yours, was that everything happened all at once. This must have been completely devastating for Job. I am sure you can relate to Job's story. One minute you're on top of the mountain enjoying life and the next minute you're down in the valley of calamity. Just like Job was determined to remain focused on the pathway, we need the same determination. No matter what roadblocks find their way onto the path we must remember that God has the power to make things better.

Reading Job's story, we see that God has the sovereignty to give blessings and take them away. "Naked I came from my mother's womb, and naked I will depart. The LORD gave and the LORD has taken away; may the name of the LORD be praised." In all this, Job did not sin by charging God with wrongdoing" (Job 1:21-22). Job remembered God's sovereignty, meaning that God possessed power to so-ever-reign. God possesses the power to allow good or bad circumstances to enter our life for a purpose. Job recognized that God was the One who allowed the calamity to enter his life. God did not create the roadblocks, Satan did. However, God allowed the roadblocks to be placed onto Job's pathway.

Remember chapter 2, "It was necessary?", there was purpose to Job's calamity. God knew the outcome. He knew that Job would make it through the tough times because He would assist him in maintaining his strength and faith. God knew that the roadblocks Satan created were not powerful enough to destroy Job's future. God had a reason for it all. In the end, Job's faith was increased. Most of all, Job's story served as an example to us to remain on our pathway even with roadblocks. "No temptation has overtaken you except what is common to mankind. And God is faithful; he will not let you be tempted beyond what you can bear. But when you are tempted, he will also provide a way out so that you can endure it" (1 Corinthians 10:12).

God said to Job in chapter 38:4-7, "Where were you when I laid the earth's foundation? Tell me, if you understand. Who marked off its dimensions? Surely you know! Who stretched a measuring line across it? On what were its footings set, or who laid its cornerstone- while the morning stars sang together and all the angels shouted for joy?"

God was reminding Job of His sovereign power. God takes care of the earth and controls what happens. Job had a choice when calamity entered his life. Either he would stop serving God or continue to trust God's pathway. Job could have decided to give up, but he decided to acknowledge God's power. Job decided to have faith in the God who laid the foundations of the earth. In my imagination I picture Job thinking to himself, "If God could create the world; surely He can fix the calamity of my life."

~Though He Slay Me Challenge~

My challenge to you is to vow that despite your circumstances of being slain, you will have faith in God. Recognize that God possesses the right to give blessings and take them away. Just like Job's story, God will be at your side giving you strength to endure. God only gives us what He knows we can handle. The best thing of all is that at the end of calamity, God gives us a double portion of blessings. We never come out empty handed when we overcome our trials.

~Life Scriptures~

"After Job had prayed for his friends, the LORD restored his fortunes and gave him twice as much as he had before. All his brothers and sisters and everyone who had known him before came and ate with him in his house. They comforted and consoled him over all the trouble the LORD had brought on him, and each one gave him a piece of silver and a gold ring" (Job 42:10-11).

"The LORD blessed the latter part of Job's life more than the former part. He had fourteen thousand sheep, six thousand camels, a thousand yoke of oxen and a thousand donkeys. And he also had seven sons and three daughters. The first daughter he named Jemimah, the second Keziah and the third Keren-Happuch. Nowhere in all the land were there found women as beautiful as Job's daughters, and their father granted them an inheritance along with their brothers. After this, Job lived a hundred and forty years; he saw his children and their children to the fourth generation. And so Job died, an old man and full of years" (Job 42:10-17).

"I have told you these things, so that in me you may have peace. In this world you will have trouble. But take heart! I have overcome the world" (John 16:33).

"But the Lord is faithful, and he will strengthen and protect you from the evil one" (2 Thessalonians 3:3).

"Be self-controlled and alert. Your enemy the devil prowls around like a roaring lion looking for someone to devour. Resist him, standing firm in the faith, because you know that your brothers throughout the world are undergoing the same kind of sufferings. And the God of all grace, who called you to his eternal glory in Christ, after you have suffered a little while, will himself restore you and make you strong, firm and steadfast" (1 Peter 5:8-10).

~Points to Ponder~

❖ Define the word slain and blessed.

❖ How does Job's story relate to your life?

❖ What life lessons can you learn from the Job's life?

❖ What scriptures support the idea that God gives you only what you can bear?

❖ What scriptures support the concept that God blesses us abundantly after we endure life's trials?

CHAPTER 9

NEBULA

Nebula is a cloud of interstellar matter (particles if you may) that is massive and widespread within Earth's outer atmosphere. This mass of interstellar matter consists of different types of gases and dust. Within Nebulae, the stars you see in the sky can form. When they are forming, they leave their surroundings in a picture of bright colors. As they form, they become very hot. High energy radiation causes the different gases, mainly hydrogen, to shine bright. Even if the stars lacked heat, their light would still shine because of the dust that surrounds them. The dust reflects many different colors. If you have the time, google pictures of Nebula to experience the amazement your eyes will behold. When you see pictures of these brightly colored arrangements in space, I want you to picture something else. I want you to picture a creator who is powerful, wise, and massive enough to create such infinite beauty.

How can such massive and brightly colored groups of dust and gas exist? How are they extravagant, massive, beautiful, and remain steady in orbit, never disappearing? If no one has brought this to your attention, may I? There is a creator who made this universe. He also created Nebulae. Where else did these things originate? How can space particles decide to form the shapes and colors that they do? Do you think that it just happens? If you took science courses growing up, do you remember the law of entropy where it says things can only go from order to disorder? Everything in this universe must go from a state of order to disorder if it's left alone. Things do not go from disorder to order.

Therefore, the law of entropy defeats what we learn about the big bang theory. Here is an example, when you don't clean your room it doesn't become clean unless you or something intervenes. If you leave the room messy it becomes more chaotic when nothing is done. Someone or something must clean it. Without an intervention the room will become worse over time. In other words, for this world to have been created I believe something, or someone, had to intervene. I believe that it was God because otherwise the pieces of the puzzles could not be put together. Can the world somehow defy the laws of physics and create itself, as it says in the big bang theory? Imagine if there is not a creator. Would there be a purpose to life?

I believe this world was created. Someone or something did intervene. We have someone who loved us enough to create us. It created a beautiful universe for us to enjoy. The laws of science testify to creation. It's up to us to see the beauty and believe that someone made it just for us. To those of us who already have faith in God, do you realize how magnificent is God? Do you understand that God is the creator of this massive universe? Have you asked God to help you through a situation, but did not believe He could?

The thing is, if you believe God is the creator of the world, how can solving your situations be harder than creating a universe? Why is it that you have so little faith in what God can do? Jeremiah 32:27, God says, "I am the Lord, the God of all mankind. Is anything too hard for me?" The question was rhetorical. The answer clearly was, no! There is nothing too hard for God. Referring to "a note from the author", I remember times when I lack faith that God can take care of my bad situations. However, with time I realize that God can do what He wants and when He wants. He is sovereign (ruler), omnipotent (all powerful), omnipresent (everywhere), omniscient (all knowing), and cannot be explained to our human mind. If He can create Nebula and this universe, then He can change your negative circumstances.

~Nebula Challenge~

The amount of heat, energy, and chemicals that are needed to create such masterpieces (Nebulae) requires more than just happenstance. Don't you think? Something must create them. Something bigger than the universe itself. A supernatural being. God. If God can create such elaborate constellations, then He can create a better life for us. He has the capability to heal us, deliver us from bad situations, and turn our sadness into gladness. The challenge is, do you believe?

Will you believe the greatness of God? I encourage you to see God on a deeper level. Search out the infinite beauties beyond your finite box. This means that you may have to google pictures of the universe and Earth. Expand your horizon to learn more about creation. Have faith to believe that the God of this massive universe has the power to help you!

~Life Scriptures~

"To the only God our Savior be glory, majesty, power and authority, through Jesus Christ our Lord, before all ages, now and forever more! Amen" (Jude

1:25).

"In the beginning God created the heaven and the earth" (Genesis 1:1).

"For in six days the LORD made the heavens and earth, the sea, and all that is in them is, but he rested on the seventh day. Therefore the LORD blessed the Sabbath day and made it holy" (Exodus 20:11).

"It will be a sign between me and the Israelites forever, for in six days the LORD made the heavens and earth, and on the seventh day he rested and was refreshed" (Exodus 31:17).

"He spreads out the northern skies over empty space; he suspends the earth over nothing" (Job 26:7).

"Where were you when I laid the earth's foundation? Tell me, if you understand" (Job 38:4).

~Points to Ponder~

- ❖ What is the creation story? Where can it be found?
- ❖ Read Genesis 1-2.
- ❖ Define the laws of the universe. This requires google. For example, the law of entropy. How do these laws relate to the creation story?
- ❖ What is the big bang theory? Why is it significant? If the big bang theory is true, what does this mean about your life?
- ❖ Can there be purpose in your life without a creator?
- ❖ In your note pad write few things about nature that hint to a creator.
- ❖ If the world was created by God, what does this mean about your life?
- ❖ Listen to the song, "You are God Alone" by Marvin Sapp.

CHAPTER 10

REJOICE OVER MY HATERS' DEFEAT

"My enemies say of me in malice, 'When will he die and in his name perish?' Whenever one comes to see me, he speaks falsely, while his heart gathers slander; then he goes out and spreads it abroad. All my enemies whisper together against me; they imagine the worst for me saying, 'A vile disease has beset him; he will never get up from the place where he lies.' Even my close friend, whom I trusted, he who shared my bread, has lifted up his heel against me" (Psalm 41:5-9 NIV).

This Psalm was written by David during a time of illness. He was on his death bed and reflected on his life. David began with Psalm 41 as he acknowledged his sinful nature (read Psalm 41). As David acknowledged his sins, he remembered the sinful nature of others towards him. He remembered how they betrayed him. Being reminded of this he recalled that he betrayed God. This betrayal was a triangle involving himself, his enemies, and God. If you betrayed one, then you betrayed the other.

When David betrayed his friends, He betrayed God. When he betrayed God, he was likely to betray his friends. It was a three-way relationship. David's enemies, including his friends, wished he died because of he betrayed them earlier on. As friends, they should have prayed he got well. They should have helped him. During his sickness he needed them. Unfortunately, they were not in sight. They left him to die in disgrace.

Thoughts of betrayal plagued David's mind while he laid on his death bed. He remembered the betrayal he committed and the betrayal of his friends towards him. No one loved him anymore. His friends become his worse enemies. No one wished him well. He had nothing left and his enemies were prospering. I imagine as David contemplated, he wanted to get well to prove everyone wrong. It's like us, we try our best to use the negative words of others to motivate our success. I imagine David fought hard to stay alive. Defeat was the last word he wanted to taste.

Have you felt that way? Do you want to prove to everyone that hated you that they were wrong about what they said? Do you want to show them what they said about you did not affect you? You want them to look at you and wish they didn't say a word. You want your success to be the worse pain they ever feel. I have been there. I believe that at some point, we all have. As time progressed David was healed from the sickness. He gained power and strength. Although his enemies wished he died, he lived. He fought through the sickness because he knew God was on his side. Instead of him being defeated, his enemies were destroyed (Psalm 38 and 41). Through his journey David recognized the betrayal of his friends, the betrayal he committed against them, and the betrayal he committed towards God.

He remembered his short comings. If you know about David, he committed adultery, sexual perversion, murder, betrayal, and more. He betrayed other people, even his most loyal servant Uriah (2 Samuel 11-12). David slept with Uriah's wife. Afterwards, she became pregnant. David decided to kill Uriah to cover his deceit. Then, he married Uriah's wife. Obviously, David knew what betrayal was because he did it himself.

Since David realized what he did, he asked God for forgiveness. He went to God to apologize. This is called repentance (sorrow for wrong acts). After asking for forgiveness, he asked God for strength. God granted him the strength he needed to heal. Even though David's enemies wanted to see him suffer because of what he did, God forgave him. God allowed him to succeed. The great news about David's story is that it signifies we can experience the same victorious outcome.

If we recognize our short comings, ask God for forgiveness, and are determined to change, we can live victorious lives. Despite the negative naysayers and haters, we can overcome our "sickness." We can experience healing. No enemy can stop us from achieving our life's goals. When God intervenes on your behalf, what was once sick becomes healthy. Your life becomes alive. Don't worry about your enemies because your enemies will reap what they have sown.

My question to you is, what will you do when your enemies begin to reap the damage they have sown? According to human thinking, the proper thing is to rejoice over their downfall. However, what is the best thing to do? Let's look at Proverbs 24:17-18, "Do not gloat when your enemy falls; when he stumbles, do not let your heart rejoice, or the Lord will see and disprove and turn his wrath away from him."

This passage reminds us that if we find ourselves gloating over the downfall of our "haters," God will spare them because of His love for everyone. As a result, our enemies will begin to prosper. They may even become more successful. Christ doesn't uphold one person over the other. He is no respecter of persons (a church cliché found in Romans 2:11). Even though someone is your enemy and will reap what they sow, God still loves them. Asking me to explain this type of love is crazy because I cannot grasp this concept. The only thing I can tell you is that this type of love is seen only with God. God designed His laws of life in such a way that not only will your enemies reap what they have sown, but you will too! If you think you are worthy to despise someone else, even if they wronged you, God will show you that you possess no authority to do so. Why? Have you not betrayed other people? Have you not done wrong to others? Don't you deserve to reap what you have sown?

You, nor your enemy, are worthy of forgiveness. Your own life has been spared by God's love. You have done wrong to others and mistreated God. The reason why you may not be suffering is because of God's mercy. His mercy gives you what you do not deserve which is forgiveness. If God decides to take His mercy from you, you would experience the same reaping as your enemies. So do not gloat in your enemy's defeat. However, boast in the forgiveness God gave to both of you. Rejoice in how God delivered you from their traps. Do not lose sight of the fact that we all deserve to reap the bad things we sow.

Praying for your enemies is a better solution to keep you on the track of success. Wanting your enemies to recognize how they hurt you is better than wishing that they die. I understand that this is hard to grasp. Trust me since I am still learning. However, the way you can do this is by asking God to fill your heart with love. As we discussed in chapter 2, it begins with forgiveness. After forgiveness we can see our need to love our enemies. When you wish the best for your enemies, you are wishing the best for yourself.

Think about it. If you are wishing the best for everyone you will automatically get the best yourself. It's like the law of attraction. What goes around, comes around. What goes up must come down. You know all those clichés we say. You reap what you sow. You sow good things, then you will reap good things. You want others to be blessed, then you will be blessed. We all would like to reap the good that we sow. We must pray that God turns our enemies mourning into gladness. Turn their wrongs into rights. Praying for your enemy is an action that lines up with a forgiving heart.

~ Rejoice Over my Hater's Defeat Challenge~

My challenge to you is when you see your enemies reaping what they sow, acknowledge that you've been spared from their traps! Remember that you have no right to gloat over their downfall. You too could be in their position if it was not for God's mercy. While remembering what God did for you, rejoice because His grace is on you. Begin praying that this grace falls on your haters. Pray that their hearts are brought back to God. Choose to rejoice in the grace of God and not the defeat of your enemies.

~Life Scriptures~

"Bless those who persecute you; bless and do not curse" (Romans 12:14).

"Do not repay anyone evil for evil" (Romans 12:17).

"Do not take revenge, my friends, but leave room for God's wrath, for it is written: 'It is mine to avenge; I will repay,' says the Lord" (Romans 12:19).

"On the contrary: 'If your enemy is hungry, feed him; if he is thirsty, give him something to drink. In doing this, you will heap burning coals on his head.' Do not be overcome by evil, but overcome evil with good" (Romans 12:20-21).

~Points to Ponder~

❖ Have you ever betrayed anyone?

❖ Who betrayed you?

❖ How is the story of David related to your life?

❖ What did you learn from reading David's story?

❖ How can you apply David's story to your life?

❖ Success is one of the greatest avengers. Why?

❖ Compare and contrast the idea of an eye for an eye with forgiveness. Which of these benefits both people?

❖ What are familiar quotes about forgiveness? Which quotes would you like to live by?

❖ Read the stories of Nelson Mandela, Mahatma Gandhi, Immaculle Ilibagiza, and Joseph (Biblical character).

CHAPTER 11

THERE I STOOD

Through all my pain,
There I stood.
Through the storm and rain,
There I stood.
When friends and loved ones left me to die,
There I stood.
Even though at times I wondered why,
There I stood.
At times I wondered if I even could, but
There I stood.
Wishing and hoping things would work out,
There I stood.
Sometimes I wondered why you walked out,
There I stood.
Even when I hated me,
There I stood.
Even when I felt God left me,
There I stood.
At times the sun was unseen by my wet eyes,
There I stood.
Hoping and wishing you would wipe my tears away,
There I stood.
Even when you knew I was up to no good,
There I stood.
With pain, hurt, anger, and shame,
There I stood.
Not knowing what was to be gained,
There I stood.
There is no way I ever believed that I would, but
There I stood.
Now, my life is brand new because
I stood.
I stood at the foot of God's throne.
I asked Him to take me back home.
I cried tears on His shoulder.

There was a deep sense it would soon be over.

He took me to a new place.

My pain He erased.

My heart is now laced with love, forgiveness, and hope.

I realize that God's word is addictive like dope.

God's word cut my heart in two.

It made me realize it's the truth.

I can attest to those who are wondering if God still cares.

I can say, "Yes, God is still right there."

Lift your head and say,

I stood all because He could!

~There I Stood Challenge~

My Challenge to you is to stand firm amid the chaos. Allow God to give you supernatural strength to endure your current hardships. I am reminded of a saying that church people quote, "When you've done all that you can, you just stand." This means that you must let go of trying to fix everything. Allow God to fix it. You must stop worrying about how you are going to make it through another day. The only thing that you need to do is remain standing firm along your life's journey. Decide that you will never sit down and quit.

~Life Scriptures~

"The LORD is my strength and my song; he has become my salvation. He is my God, and I will praise him, my father's God, and I will exalt him" (Exodus 15:2).

"Look to the LORD and his strength; seek his face always" (1 Chronicles 16:11).

"Do not grieve, for the joy of the LORD is your strength" (Nehemiah 8:10).

"Some trust in chariots and some in horses, but we trust in the name of the LORD our God. They are brought to their knees and fall, but we rise up and stand firm" (Psalm 20:7-8).

"The Lord is my light and my salvation; whom shall I fear? The Lord is the stronghold of my life; of whom shall I be afraid?" (Psalm 27:1).

"The LORD is the strength of his people, a fortress of salvation for his anointed one" (Psalm 28:8).

"God is our refuge and strength, an ever-present help in trouble" (Psalm 46:1).

"But I will sing of your strength, in the morning I will sing of your love; for you are my fortress, my refuge in times of trouble" (Psalm 59:16).

"Search for the Lord and for his strength; continually seek him" (Psalm 105:4, NKJV).

~Points to Ponder~

❖ Reflecting on your life, how do you make it through tough times?
❖ What helps you?
❖ How does God help us? Write down supporting scriptures.
❖ Define the words strength, stand, and, firm. How do these support the above poem?
❖ In a group, discuss some of the toughest times of your life.
❖ Share with other women tips of how you overcame these obstacles.

CHAPTER 12

SEASONS OF LIFE

There will be times when life unfolds like a rose in full bloom. You won't have any worries. The sun will shine its light just for you. As time passes, those good days will turn into bad days. The rose pedals will wither. The sun will lose its glow. I have experienced both good and bad days. Some days my life is sunny side up. Other days it's sunny side down. All these different days, I call seasons. Every woman experiences different seasons of life.

Winter...

Some women are in their winter season. It's a cold, dry, and dying season. Nothing in life is working for your benefit. Life is crazy. You can't find peace. There is doubt that new life circumstances will bloom. You are having hardships, difficulties, distractions, droughts, and setbacks to accomplish your purpose.

Spring...

Other women are in their spring season. The weather is getting warmer. Life is beginning to bloom. Summer is right around the corner. You see a better life on the horizon. You're blossoming into your dreams, goals, and/or purpose.

Summer...

There are women who are in the season of summer. Often, we view summer as the best season of all. Life is going perfect. Everything and everyone are alive and active. You are fulfilling your dreams, goals, and visions. However, after summer comes fall.

Fall...

Lastly, we have women in their fall season. A season where the colors of the leaves are beautiful. However, the leaves are slowly drying up because winter is on the way. There is much color (signifying a variety of goodness) in your life, but the warmth of summer is fading. The cold wind of winter is beginning. Just like fall has bouts of cold and hot weather, you have bouts of sadness (cold) and happiness (hot). It's a time for growth, maturity, and pruning.

There are so many different seasons that enter our lives at different stages. Ask any woman. She'll have a preference which season is her favorite and which she hates the most. No matter what her preference is, each season will be a part of her life. Each season will serve a purpose. We cannot control which season enters. When a season enters our life, we must endure its stay and learn from the effects. Currently, what season are you in?

Winter...

Are you in your winter months? No one is to be found. You are alone. Nothing is working according to your plans. As a result, you're depressed. You ask yourself, "Why me?" You're searching for healing and guidance. In your mind, this is the worst season of life. Contrary to what you may believe about winter, it does serve a purpose. Those winter months bring you into a deeper connection with your creator. The cold of the winter causes you to look for warmth. This warmth is found in the arms of the One who made you. Winter is a unique season. I believe during the depressing times of life; we connect to God on an intimate level. He is all we have during those times. God becomes everything to us. We depend on His supernatural power during the winter seasons.

We find ourselves seeking His purpose for our life. We find ourselves wanting to learn more. During these months we allow our soul to be comforted by His' words. He's all that you can rely on during these cold months of life. The great thing about the winter is that you gain a sense of security in God. An internal peace is granted when we go through difficult times. "You will keep in perfect peace those whose minds are steadfast, because they trust in you" (Isaiah 26:3). During winter, your faith and intimacy with God escalates. Towards the end of this season, faith in God's power is developed. You will know that God pulled you out of your negative circumstances. Don't forget, eventually spring enters.

Spring...

After winter, comes the season of spring. During your spring months there are many transitions that will happen. Just as the earth is transitioning into new life, so will you. You will wonder which "flowers" will bloom in your life and which will fade away. You will want the spring to hurry and reveal the oncoming destination (summer) for your life. You will know that summer is around the corner and winter is finally fading. Newness is on the horizon. The cold wind of winter is passing away.

However, the heat of summer has yet to be felt. The season is still in transition. Your life is between winter and summer. During this season you will find yourself asking God to rush the transition, so you can enter the summer heat. God will say, "be patient." God wants you to experience the beauty of transitioning. Do not rush through your blossoming phase. Every rose must undergo a blooming phase. Too often we ignore God's advice for spring and ask for summer. When we ignore God's advice to enjoy the transition, we fail to see our growth process.

We skip out on experiencing how the sun peeks in and out of the clouds onto our cheeks. We overlook how the flowers (life's situations) are transitioning in their beauty. Even though we understand the beauty of transformation, we think summer is better than winter. Forgetting that summer while it's a wonderful season, can sometimes be too hot. Be careful what you wish for, right?

Those of us who decide to enjoy the beauty of transitioning don't mind waiting until summer arrives. During the waiting process you'll learn to depend on the faith you developed during the winter season. You'll believe that your circumstances are getting ready to change. The good times of life are beginning. God's favor is being poured out. You have come to understand that God brought you through the winter (hardships), is transitioning you through the spring (transformation), and will propel you into summer (blessings). Spring is the season where you realize that God parted your Red Sea (read Exodus 15). You're walking through the parted sea of life's struggles. One day you will reach the other side.

Summer…

As the transition comes to an end, you will cross over to the other side where summer begins. The deadness of winter is gone. The semi-summer of spring has evaded. It's full-blown summertime. The trees of life will be full of bright green leaves. All of life's flowers will be in full bloom. The sun will shine. You will be ready to take on the heat. At this time of life nothing will convince you that God didn't take you through the harshness of the winter. You will find yourself basking in the glow of the sun (son of God, Christ). God's blessings will overflow in your life. Everyone and everything around you will be made new.

During summer life is vibrant. The drum of your heart plays to an upbeat rhythm. Your smile shines bright from the depth of your relief. You are completely transformed and ready to shine. One thing you may notice during summer is that sometimes it can get too hot. In other words, the many blessing and attention you receive can become overwhelming. That's when you should cool off in the refreshing water of life (God's word/presence). As the water hits the heat of your skin, it will glisten. It will cool the effects of the scorching heat.

Regardless of it getting too hot, you'll realize that you are free from the bondage of your winter clothes that used to weigh you down (life's burdens). Your soul is light allowing you to soar into your destiny. Everything you lost during the battles of winter (joy, peace, youthfulness, smile, heavenly glow) has been restored. At this point of life, you have grounded faith to know that God can turn bad situations into a good one. You know that God will provide for you. You realize He loves you in a special way, but how long will summer last? How long will you continue to win life's battles?

Fall…

Seasons always change. After summer, comes fall. The fall season serves as another type of transitioning. Instead of transitioning from bad days to great days, you will transition from great days to bad days. This is a tough season. Who wants to transition from summer to winter? The faith you developed during the winter, spring, and summer months, are needed during this time. The rays of the sun will begin to fade. The trees and flowers will wilt. The weather starts with a slight chill. Everyone around you retreats into the solitude of the indoors.

During fall loneliness takes root in your life. It seems you're walking alone. You'll wonder why summer ended so fast. Summer now is simply a dream. The green leaves that once hung from life's tree begins to turn colors. The colors are beautiful in their arrangements, but it means the leaves are slowly dying inside. The leaves remind you of yourself. You are outwardly beautiful from the enjoyment of summer, but inside you are losing a grip on life.

What's happening? What's coming next? Why is God taking everything away that He restored in the summer months? Why is He allowing you to transition back into winter? You don't want the lushness summer to fade, but it does. Winter is approaching. The life to death and the death to life process has re-started, as it does each year. Again, you find yourself asking God for guidance. You plead for summer to last longer. During the fall season you must keep the faith you had during the summer. Remember the previous seasons and how you endured. Remember what God did for you each season. God has not left you. He is not going to leave you stranded during the fall. "The LORD himself goes before you and will be with you; he will never leave you nor forsake you. Do not be afraid; do not be discouraged" (Deuteronomy 31:8). Remember that no season lasts forever. Even though you will transition into the winter; spring and summer will arrive. Have faith that God is in control of each season.

~Seasons of Life Challenge~

My challenge to you today is to accept whatever season of life that you're in. Whether it's your favorite or not, each seasonal process serves a purpose. The purpose may be for spiritual growth, personal growth, or life's lessons. Either way, there is a reason for the season! Don't overlook one season for anticipation of the next. Hidden beauties are found among dying trees and blooming flowers. Embrace every transition that befalls you. Allow growth to take place during each transition as you move along this lifelong season of womanhood.

~Life Scriptures and Quotes~

"Every person placed in our life, whether for a season, reason, or lifetime, is a blessing from God! The objective is to figure out why they were there. In each circumstance there is a lesson learned and a blessing gained. Don't hate the season because all seasons must change. Change is good so the next season can enter!" – Stephanneth Adams

"There is a time for everything, and a season for every activity under the heavens: a time to be born and a time to die, a time to plant and a time to uproot, a time to kill and a time to heal, a time to tear down and a time to build, a time to weep and a time to laugh, a time to mourn and a time to dance, a time to scatter stones and a time to gather them, a time to embrace and a time to refrain from embracing, a time to search and a time to give up, a time to keep and a time to throw away, a time to tear and a time to mend, a time to be silent and a time to speak, a time to love and a time to hate, a time for war and a time for peace. What do workers gain from their toil? I have seen the burden God has laid on the human race. He has made everything beautiful in its time. He has also set eternity in the human heart; yet no one can fathom what God has done from beginning to end. I know that there is nothing better for people than to be happy and to do good while they live. That each of them may eat and drink, and find satisfaction in all their toil—this is the gift of God. I know that everything God does will endure forever; nothing can be added to it and nothing taken from it. God does it so that people will fear him. Whatever is has already been, and what will be has been before; and God will call the past to account. And I saw something else under the sun: In the place of judgment—wickedness was there, in the place of justice—wickedness was there. I said to myself, "God will bring into judgment both the righteous and the wicked, for there will be a time for every activity, a time to judge every deed." I also said to myself, "As for humans, God tests them so that they may see that they are like the animals. Surely the fate of human beings is like that of the animals; the same fate awaits them both: As one dies, so dies the other. All have the same breath; humans have no advantage over animals. Everything is meaningless. All go to the same place; all come from dust, and to dust all return. Who knows if the human spirit rises upward and if the spirit of the animal goes down into the earth?" So I saw that there is nothing better for a person than to enjoy their work, because that is their lot. For who can bring them to see what will happen after them?" (Ecclesiastes 3).

~Points to Ponder~

❖ Currently, which season of life are you in?

❖ How can you transition through this season?

❖ What helps you cope during this season?

❖ Reading Ecclesiastes 3. How does this relate to your life? What did you learn from the reading?

❖ List tips to deal with the transitional seasons of fall and spring.

❖ Discuss with other women the idea of "seasons." Share your current season with each other. How is your process of transition is going? Share wisdom you learned from the process.

Chapter 13

The Secrets of Abuse

Cuddled over in a corner I sat and wondered.
Why am I here?
Why do I stay with him?
My life seems so dim.
Someone tell me where did this start?
Where did it all begin?
I remember it started with just one sin.
One day he, yep, I said him.
He came into my room when the lights were dim.
Mother never knew him the way that I did.
He came into my room, where we 'chimmy chim chimmed.'
We 'chimmy chim chimmed' the night away.
We 'chimmy chim chimmed' until my skin turned grey.
Grey as the dark sky at night.
Tears running until I could no longer fight.
Fight him off me, I did try to do.
Nothing would work because he'd beat me until I turned blue.
Mother never questioned my tears or the appearance of my fears.
She only worried that he'd leave her.
And what she could do to please her, her man.
My father he was supposed to be.
Instead he was only an enemy.
A wolf in sheep's clothing.
Yes, that's what he was.
Now I'm drowning deep in relational muck, all just because.
Because of him I have entered a cycle of sin.
Sin, abuse, and disgrace are written on my face.
Will I ever break free from the chains he placed?
Will I ever see myself as God sees me?
What does a woman like me do?
I have no one or nowhere to run to.
If I run, he will find me.
When he does, he will confine me again, to this corner.

This corner where I sit and think.
This corner where my heart sinks.
Free from both enemies is what I need to be.
Lord, I'm making my plea.
When you get me out of here,
I do swear that I will run to you.
Who else do I have, but you?
Mother didn't even care to believe what was true.
If I could run and tell every young lady like me what to do,
I would tell them to run, run, run away.
Don't stay young lady.
Don't stay with him.
He will only make your life dim.
Dim as the darkest, blackest, night.
Run, run, run, and don't stay.
God will make a way.
A way of escape.
He will be your hero with a cape.
Don't stay like I did because of what my father did.
I only found that it was stupid.
Yes, yes, you do have wings.
You have wings that can fly beyond the big blue skies.
So, run I say, and save your day.
When you get to where you're going remember me.
Remember my story.
Remember your story.
Remember our story and how you were set free.
Tell every young girl.
Tell every old one too.
Let them know just what to do.
Don't forget to tell them that no matter what happens, God still loves you!

~Secrets of Abuse Challenge~

My challenge to you today is to decide to save your life! Refuse to live any longer with less than what you deserve! Visit www.rainn.com for information about abuse agencies and assistance. There is a way of escape. Call your local abuse agency, church, or primary healthcare provider for assistance. These agencies are there to help you plan a strategic way of escape. They will assist you in rebuilding your life and self-esteem. Call today. Although I did not experience the pain of sexual or physical abuse. I know its effects from the women I encounter. It's so common. The hurt is real. My family was touched by domestic violence when I found out my cousin, she was around 28 years old, was shot to death by her boyfriend. Her two young boys found her dead in the kitchen. I was much younger at the time and did not grasp the full meaning of the situation.

Looking back, I realize how common is domestic violence. Not only domestic or sexual violence, but emotional abuse. Emotional abuse can be difficult to identify. Sometimes when it is identified you are so wrapped into it that it is hard to break free. I have encountered emotional abuse in a previous romantic relationship. Boy, does it take a toll on you. The best way to prevent emotional abuse is to know the signs! When entering any type of relationship watch for its signs. At the first sign that the person is emotionally abusive, tell them what Beyoncé said, "To the left. To the left".

~Life Scriptures~

"Our God is a God who saves; from the Sovereign Lord comes escape from death" (Psalm 68:20).

"In this same way, husbands ought to love their wives as their own bodies. He who loves his wife loves himself. After all, no one ever hated their own body, but they feed and care for their body, just as Christ does the church" (Ephesians 5:28-29).

"Get rid of all bitterness, rage and anger, brawling and slander, along with every form of malice" (Ephesians 4:31).

"Husbands, love your wives and do not be harsh with them" (Colossians 3:19).

"In the same way, you husbands must give honor to your wives. Treat her with understanding as you live together. She may be weaker than you are, but she is your equal partner in God's gift of new life. If you don't treat her as you should, your prayers will not be heard" (1Peter 3:7).

"The mouth of the righteous is a fountain of life, but the mouth of the wicked

72

conceals violence. Hatred stirs up conflict, but love covers over all wrongs" (Proverbs 10:11-12).

"My dear brothers and sisters, take note of this: Everyone should be quick to listen, slow to speak and slow to become angry, because human anger does not produce the righteousness that God desires" (James 1:19-20).

~Points to Ponder~

- ❖ Have you found yourself in a cycle of abuse?
- ❖ Are you currently in an abusive relationship? Evaluate why you are staying.
- ❖ You are worth more than bumps and bruises, so is this person worth you dying?
- ❖ Where did the abuse start? For example, was it childhood, teen years, or your first relationship? Discover where it began and who was the source of the abuse.
- ❖ As you are journaling, I want you to think about how you can stop the cycle.
- ❖ What is your escape plan?
- ❖ In your note pad list 5 abuse agencies and/or crises hotlines.
- ❖ How can you use your story to warn other women?
- ❖ Did you forgive the person who first abused you? Review chapter 2.
- ❖ Did you forgive yourself? It was not your fault.
- ❖ In your note pad list 5 reasons why you need to leave the person who is abusing you, 5 ways you plan to leave, 5 goals you plan to complete when you leave, and 5 things that can happen if you do not leave.
- ❖ Visit www.rainn.com for information on abuse.

CHAPTER 14

BEING PREGNANT IS NOT MY END

Pre-marital pregnancy is the act of getting pregnant before marriage. At least that is what we'll call it. It is commonplace in so many of our lives. It's almost expected to become pregnant before having a committed relationship. While we're on this topic, I can't help telling you about the journey of a young girl. She was around twenty-two at the time. I remember she fell in love with a guy who did not love her. One day she became ill. Her body began to work differently, and things were out of whack.

Her stomach had massive cramps. Her bleeding was more than moderate, and the blood was malodorous. Something was wrong. Something was out of place. She wondered, am I pregnant? Did I have an incomplete miscarriage? Did I contract a sexually transmitted disease? What can it be? Struggling with the thought of being pregnant, she decided to take a pregnancy test. What type of thoughts do you think ran through her mind as she searched the aisles of the grocery store?

There she was in the fertility aisle by herself looking for a product that would give her an answer she needed to know. The answer would change her life forever. As she stood there staring at the HCG strips, what was she thinking? Was she wondering what was next in her life? Was she wondering how was she placed in this situation? Did she feel sorry for herself? Was her level of self-esteem dropping by the minute? Did she wonder how she would raise a possible child? Did she wonder why the baby's father was somewhere else without a care? Was her future a glimpse of failure and disappointment? Was she thinking that she had failed herself, God, and her family?

There she was alone in the aisle of the grocery store wanting to find out if her life would be drastically changed. Her life was on the line. Her dreams were on the line. Her self-esteem was on the line. What was she to do? Where was she to go? Who was she to turn to? If the test turned out to be positive, how could she face the shame? How could she turn to her family and explain the ordeal? How would she break the news to her lost lover? How could she place herself before God and tell Him she still wanted to be His daughter? What would be her life's purpose and that of the child?

Just like the story of this young lady, there are similar stories. Many women find ourselves in situations we never imagined. So many women, young and old, make the mistake of allowing ourselves to be placed in circumstances that change our lives forever. Wondering how I got here, when did I get here, and why did I get here, are often the thoughts that consume our minds. Maybe currently you are going through a similar situation or know someone who is. You're asking, where do I go from here? What should I do?

For the young lady in the story above, her answers to those questions were eventually given. It turned out that she wasn't in the situation she thought. However, it was still a problem that needed to be resolved. Despite not testing positive for pregnancy, she wasn't exempt from the feelings that many women experience going through the same thing. She felt the pain. She felt the disappointment and shame. Anyone can find themselves in a place of unwanted pregnancy.

I'm not talking about a wanted or planned pregnancy. Nor am I speaking about pregnancy resulting from the love that a husband and wife share. I'm talking about a surprised pregnancy. I am referring to falling into the adversaries' trap of fornication, without commitment, leading to a situation that can hinder your future. I am talking about pregnancy outside the laws of God, forcing you to wonder whether you should get rid of the baby. I am talking about being shamefully pregnant. This can hinder your vision for a brighter future and cause you to isolate yourself from the world.

The truth is that you don't have to hide anymore. Your shame is going to be erased. Right here and now. Today is the day to confess and embrace your situation. This is the day to confess your shame, mishaps, and flaws. Yes, being pregnant outside of lifelong commitment can destroy your future. Your life will never be the same. Your self-esteem will be damaged. Your baby's father may never be there to help. You now have a great responsibility. Most of all, you have placed a brick wall between you and God.

However, by confessing your flaws your shame can be removed. With confession comes freedom! With confession the shackles that hold you down can be broken. Your shame can be erased, and your purpose fulfilled. Your needs can be met, and your joy restored. Your secrets can become testimonies. Your lost love can be revived. Your parents can be made proud. Your friends can be replenished. Your virtue can be restored. Your name can become great. Your sins can be forgiven. This all can happen if you accept that confession is good for your soul!

Don't allow yourself to live in the shame of what happened. Don't allow yourself to walk around with secrets that hinder your prosperity. Don't allow yourself to be pushed further away from God. Don't refuse to be made whole. God still has a purpose for your life. God has a purpose for not only yours, but for the life you are carrying. Remember the sin is never in the outcome (the baby), it was the pre-marital sex. God hated the act, (because He wants better for you) but loves you!

God loves you and your baby. He doesn't love the fact you didn't allow Him to fulfill your needs. God didn't love the fact that you chose someone else over Him. Instead of true love, you chose false security. That is what God hated. When we choose false love, we accept everything that is anti-God because He is love. Choosing whatever is the opposite of true love is a sin and leaves us damaged. Therefore, the sin was in the act and not the outcome.

People will try to tell you that the outcome is a sin, but that's a lie. They will try to point the finger, but they'll never open the door of their own closet. Dear sister, never allow anyone to place shame on you. Many people who point a finger at your shame also have done the same thing you have. The only difference is that no one may know their secret. They live in the secrecy of pre-marital sex. However, you have been set free from the secrecy of your pregnancy. Let the finger pointers live in shame. Let your secret be a testimony of God's love towards you. God has blessed you with a bundle of joy to nurture, cherish, and mold. Don't give up on God because God has not given up on you.

~Being Pregnant is Not My End Challenge~

If you've found yourself struggling with the secrecy or shame of being pregnant, I encourage you to admit the situation. Allow God's love to empower you. Allow God to direct your life and that of your baby. Be encouraged that everything will work out for your benefit. God has given life to you. Don't waste it walking around in shame. Share your story with the world. That is the only way something good can happen.

By accepting the situation purpose can be brought into your life. Find other people who will help. Find a shelter for pregnant women or other types of prenatal assistance. Whatever you need to do to win, like Nike says, "Just do it!"

~Life Scriptures~

"For I know the plans I have for you," declares the LORD, "plans to prosper you and not to harm you, plans to give you hope and a future"" (Jeremiah

29:11).

"And we know that in all things God works for the good of those who love him, who have been called according to his purpose" (Romans 8:28).

"Yet you brought me out of the womb; you made me trust in you even at my mother's breast" (Psalm 22:9).

"He will love you and bless you and increase your numbers. He will bless the fruit of your womb, the crops of your land-your grain, new wine and oil-the calves of your herds and the lambs of your flocks in the land that he swore to your forefathers to give you" (Deuteronomy 7:13).

"Though an army besiege me, my heart will not fear; though war break out against me, even then I will be confident" (Psalm 27:3).

"Children are a gift from the LORD; they are a reward from him" (Psalm 127:3).

"The LORD appeared to us in the past, saying: "I have loved you with an everlasting love; I have drawn you with unfailing kindness. I will build you up again, and you, Virgin Israel, will be rebuilt. Again you will take up your timbrels and go out to dance with the joyful. Again you will plant vineyards on the hills of Samaria; the farmers will plant them and enjoy their fruit""" (Jeremiah 31:3-5).

~Points to Ponder~

In your note pad answer the following questions:

❖ What is the reason why you look for intimacy through sex?

❖ Why did you have sex with someone without a marital commitment? How does sex without a commitment impact your life?

❖ How will pregnancy impact your life? When faced with the issue of an unwanted pregnancy, how can women overcome their shame?

❖ What do you fear most about pregnancy?

❖ Begin learning the steps to having a healthy pregnancy. Develop a relationship with an OB provider. Early prenatal care is important for a healthy pregnancy!

CHAPTER 15

MY FLESH, MY MASTER

Our desire for sexual intimacy is one of the greatest threats to our spiritual growth. We were created for life-long intimacy with a beloved mate. However, life has made it less promising to find a spouse. Finding a way to fulfill our sexual needs outside of marriage is the norm. You're probably thinking why does this matter? It matters because sex is powerful. If it wasn't then why would we desire to have it, unless you're a Nun. Sex is not bad. Don't think that I will say that because I will not. Sex is very good! It was designed by our creator, so why would it be bad? Its beautiful because it connects people in the most intimate way.

What we don't realize is that fulfilling our sexual desires outside of marriage has negative effects. We do our best to think that it's not true, but it is. Let's talk. Fornication is a word in the Bible to describe the act of pre-marital sex. Self-gratification (or masturbation) is also a term used to describe the act of sexually pleasing ourselves. Considering both terms, a person can conclude that acts of fornication and self-pleasure means that you either have sex with a person who is not your spouse or with yourself. I don't know about you but, breaking down those terms is powerful to me!

A person manipulates their mind and body to arrive at an orgasmic state, by themselves or with a person with whom they have no commitment. Most psychologist and scientist state that this is normal, however when it negatively interferes with your life or relationship it's a problem. The question is, can you fornicate or masturbate without it negatively affecting how you function or your relationships? Sex shapes who we are and our relationship with the opposite sex. It's a vital part of our lives. Our sexual appetite was given to us by God. How we curve this appetite can be rewarding or detrimental. Many of us find ourselves confused on how to positively curve our sexual desire. We find ourselves seeking self-pleasure, promiscuity, or sexual fantasy.

Many women are trying to achieve emotional and sexual satisfaction whether it's through fornication or masturbation. We find ways to experience sexual pleasure. The problem is that the self-pleasure we seek is temporary. It leaves us emotionally drained. We conjure mental fantasies, do away with our spiritual energy, and use our physical energy to find climax. After we reach climax and experience relief, reality sets back in. We did not experience a sexual high with a person who is committed to us forever. So, you withdraw from the fantasy world. It's almost like daydreaming and being hit with a bat back into reality. The "love" you just made was false. Deep down you want to experience something deeper. For Christians, we realize that it pushes us away from intimacy with God. This leads us to feel guilty, shameful, lonely, and unworthy. You become frustrated and lonelier which furthers your reliance on negatively pleasing yourself. A cycle is created that is hard to break. It can't even be stopped just because we get married because it becomes an addiction.

Why do we have self-pleasing desires? No matter how cliché this sounds, it's our enemy (Satan). As we discussed throughout this book, Satan has many deceitful tactics. His plans are always the opposite of the things we were created to do. Satan's plans bring destruction, sadness, and frustration. In terms of our sexuality, he finds ways to make us dependent on things opposite of God. Where God wants us to experience lifelong monogamous sex with the person we love, the devil wants us to have sex with anyone at any time. God wants us to save our sexuality as a gift for someone who will love us, but the devil wants us to carelessly use our sexuality.

Sex is a pleasurable gift given to us by God. It is something special and unique. It joins lovers together in the most intimate way. Think of it as a secret between two lovers. No one else joins in their pleasure. It's a "you and I" thing. It's two people selflessly pleasing each other's sexual appetites. When fornication, derogatory thoughts, or masturbation come into play, you destroy the concept of the lover's secret. Sex no longer is special. It becomes something that you do. When losing sight of its value, our full potential to climax can be hindered. We also can develop selfish desires, decreased pleasure, and failed intimacy.

These are the spiritual and emotional tolls, but what about biological. Biologically speaking, our bodies were created for survival and reproduction. Our biological clocks are always ticking. As women, our bodies constantly tell us to find a man and make babies. Our genetic material needs to survive, right? God created us to reproduce, a life-giving gift. It's a part of human nature to be sexual, fruitful, and multiply. "God blessed them and said to them, 'Be fruitful and increase in number; fill the earth and subdue it'" (Genesis 1:28). Sexual intimacy is the perfect way to fulfill this biological role.

Let's look a little closer at this text. It says that God blessed the sexual union between the man and woman. He wanted them to enjoy sex and use it to create people. It did not say that He created it to be performed outside of a joined union or alone. We cannot be fruitful by having sex outside of these boundaries. The world of fantasy goes deep. It seeps into the depths of who we are. It shifts our sexual desires, appetite, and mentality. Fantasy can curve your appetite in a detrimental way. A way you may never realize. I want you to think about the things I said. Think about how curving your appetite in the wrong way can affect your emotional, sexual, and social health.

The devil seeks to tempt you in all aspects of your life, even your sexuality. One of the most effective ways he tempts us is through secrets. You know, "Netflix and chill", welcome to the dungeon, basement pornography, and/or sex trafficking. Have you ever realized that its rare someone is open about doing these things? Satan loves to tempt us to do things that no one else would find out which opens the door for addiction. Secret sins cause us to think that you will not experience consequences. However, God knows.

So many issues happen from what seems like a simple self-relieving act. Giving you more detail about this topic won't do any good because it's most likely something you don't want to talk about. You, God, and/or your lover(s), are the only ones that know how your flesh masters (controls) your life. It will not do any good to read an entire chapter about the effects of fornication/masturbation when you think it's not a problem. How can God help someone with a secret? It requires admittance like all other addictions.

~My Flesh, My Master Challenge~

I challenge you to admit your sexual mishaps. Take the time to learn about the biological, psychological, and spiritual effects of fornication and masturbation. Admit your problem to God. Find a trustworthy person or a support group that can support you through this challenge. Secrets only have power when left unsaid. The moment the secret is shared it no longer has power. Don't allow your sexual appetites to control your life. Take back your God-given sexuality.

~Life Scriptures~

"Flee from sexual immorality. All other sins a person commits are outside the body, but whoever sins sexually, sins against their own body" (1 Corinthians 6:18).

"Therefore confess your sins to each other and pray for each other so that you may be healed. The prayer of a righteous man is powerful and effective" (James 5:16).

"If we confess our sins, he is faithful and just and will forgive us our sins and purify us from all unrighteousness" (1 John 1:9).

"Do you not know that your bodies are members of Christ himself? Shall I then take the members of Christ and unite them with a prostitute? Never! Do you not know that he who unites himself with a prostitute is one with her in body? For it is said, "The two will become one flesh" (1 Corinthians 6:15-16).

"For this reason a man will leave his father and mother and be united to his wife, and the two will become one flesh." This is a profound mystery—but I am talking about Christ and the church" (Ephesians 5:31-32).

"Flee from sexual immorality. All other sins a person commits are outside the body, but whoever sins sexually, sins against their own body" (1 Corinthians 6:18).

"You have heard that it was said to the people long ago, 'You shall not murder, and anyone who murders will be subject to judgment.' But I tell you that anyone who is angry with a brother or sister will be subject to judgment. Again, anyone who says to a brother or sister, 'Raca,' is answerable to the court. And anyone who says, 'You fool!' will be in danger of the fire of hell" (Matthew 5:21-22).

"But mark this: There will be terrible times in the last days. People will be lovers of themselves, lovers of money, boastful, proud, abusive, disobedient to their parents, ungrateful, unholy, without love, unforgiving, slanderous, without self-control, brutal, not lovers of the good, treacherous, rash, conceited, lovers of pleasure rather than lovers of God— having a form of godliness but denying its power. Have nothing to do with such people" (2 Timothy 3:1-5).

"So whether you eat or drink or whatever you do, do it all for the glory of God" (1 Corinthians 10:31).

"This means that anyone who belongs to Christ has become a new person. The old life is gone; a new life has begun" (2 Corinthians 5:17, NLT).

~Points to Ponder~

❖ STEPS in breaking an addiction
   1. Ask God for guidance.
   2. Admit your problem.
   3. Acknowledge why you fornicate or masturbate.
   4. Learn the effects each has.
   5. Make a choice to change.
   6. Enlist help from trustworthy persons (professional).
   7. Involve friends and family in your journey.
   8. Remove yourself from barriers to your change.
   9. Change your current routine.
   10. Reward yourself.

❖ Define the words sex, fornication, and masturbation?

❖ List Bible verses that talk about sexual intimacy?

❖ What are some emotional and spiritual effects of pre-marital sex, marital-based sex, and masturbation?

❖ How has sexual perversion negatively affected your life?

❖ Is love selfish or selfless? How does masturbation/fornication coincide with the definition of love and selflessness?

❖ Discuss with a group your thoughts about this chapter.

❖ Define what is a soul-tie.

❖ In your note pad write about what you learned.

CHAPTER 16

IMAGINE ME

Imagine me free from the pain.
No longer wondering what I can gain.

Free from guilt that built this quilt.
A quilt that hides and isolates me.

Isolated from the rest of the world because life makes me hurl.
I feel sick.

Sick to my stomach to the point that I plummet.
I plunge down, falling.

I sink down deeper and deeper into the muck.
I wonder, what luck?

What luck do I have for a brighter future?
Tell me because my heart needs sutures.

I need to be sutured from my head to my toes.
You can't imagine the hurt and woe.

The woe I feel.
Yet to be healed.

Healed from the pain of my past.
I often ask God, how long will this last?

How long will you allow me to stay here?
Stay here in this prison built out of fear.

Fear that all the bad will never end.
Fear that my enemies will never see me win.

Will I ever conquer my world?

Or will I die from my own sword?

The sword is the words of death I speak.
I speak them over my life.

Take me away.
Why keep me here?
Just take me away.

I can't believe life will be better.
So, I keep imagining myself free.

I keep dreaming of being free from all insecurities.
Free from the baggage, pain, and strife.

Free from being hurt.
Free from the lies.

I imagine myself free.
Free to fly.
Free to soar.
Free to grow closer to the Lord.

As I imagine myself free, I feel your hand guiding me.
Guiding me to the place of your resurrection.
Guiding me where you performed the greatest intercession.

You guide me to the place where you shed your blood.
You turn to me and say,
My child this was the day.

This was the day that I died for you.
I bore stripes for you to no longer feel blue.

You have no reason to fall.
You have a reason to get up.

Here I am my child.

I can take the pain away.

No longer imagine being free,
but understand that you have been set free this very day.

~Imagine me Challenge~

Imagining yourself being free is difficult when life has thrown you chains. The weight of our circumstances causes us to feel defeated. We speak defeat into our lives and spiritual being. We entangle ourselves in negativity and allow ourselves to become trapped. We are human. It's what we do.

The only way to break out of this mindset is to let God in. We must allow Him to speak to our hearts. We must allow Him to speak restoration into our lives. We must accept His thoughts about us to realize our value. Through daily heart-to-heart conversations with God (meditation), we can understand why we're created. Reading the Bible can help us learn about our beauty.

Talking to God is easier than we think. It's not a bunch of "jibber jabber" or rhetoric. It's sincere heart-to-heart conversation. God knows that we get frustrated. He knows we are upset, sad, depressed, and everything else. God's not bothered by us expressing our deepest concerns. He knows that life is difficult. It is up to us to talk about what He already knows.

My challenge is to have a daily talk with God. Let Him know your concerns. Talk about what hurts you, makes you cry, upset, and what you desire. He will listen. Watch for things to change in your life.

~Life Scriptures~

"Then you will know the truth, and the truth will set you free" (John 8:32).

"The tongue has the power of life and death, and those who love it will eat its fruit" (Proverbs 18:21).

"Keep your tongue from evil and your lips from telling lies" (Psalm 34:13).

"Before a word is on my tongue you, LORD, know it completely" (Psalm 139:4).

"Be strong and take heart, all you who hope in the LORD" (Psalm 31:24).

"May the God of hope fill you with all joy and peace as you trust in him, so that you may overflow with hope by the power of the Holy Spirit" (Romans 15:13).

~Points to Ponder~

- How do you relate to this poem?
- What are painful areas of your life? How do you cope with the pain?
- Speaking negative words causes us to think negatively. How can you stop?
- What scriptures talk about life and death being in the power of our tongue?
- What scriptures discuss positive thinking/faith?
- How can these scriptures help you live a better life?
- Listen to the song, "Imagine Me" by Kirk Franklin. Make this song your week's motivation.
- Schedule a daily meditation with God. During this time talk about your heart's desires.

A Woman's Preparation for Marital Destination

Chapter 17

The Love I longed for

Wishing and hoping that you love me.
Or, do I need to love me?

Praying my walls to be conquered by you.
These feelings make me unworthy and blue.

These walls cause me to grow away.
Far from your love.
Far from your touch.

Sometimes I wonder how much.
How much do you love me?
How much do you care?
They say, You're always there.

How can I trust them?
How can I know You're real?
Can I go based on the feelings I feel?

My love is locked.
Locked away to never escape.
I hide under my self-sufficient cape.

Self-strength is my tool to fight.
Fight for my rights to soar high.
But life passes by.

Passing by quick causing me to feel seasick.
Nauseated from the thoughts of wanting to be found.
Can I be found by You?
Can I let go of self-strength to be loved by You?

They say You're the best.

How best can that be?
Should I taste and see?

Right now, no one else can help.
They talk about who they depend on.
So, I'll lean on a man who knows His name.

A name with power to break chains.
Power to take away pain.

I'll try this name today and date someone new.
Someone who'll be true.

True of His word and character.
Someone who brings the heart laughter.

So, break down these walls.
Make the fears fall.

Fall in love is what I want to do.
To fall in love is what I pursue.
To fall in love with God is a dream come true.

So, I ask you to break down these walls.
Soothe the longing in my soul.
Be the love I long for.

~The Love I long for Challenge~

Your challenge is before seeking love from anyone else, develop a personal connection with God. To do this we have to ask God to breakdown our walls of past hurt, pain, anger, and self-strength. Walls that aren't torn down before entering a godly connection can destroy the relationship. Past hurts and regrets can split people apart. You only have one heart. Don't let its walls get in the way of experiencing true love. The second part of the challenge is to allow God to be your matchmaker.

❖ **The love I long for process:**
      1. Confront your past relationship mistakes.

2. Accept the help of a higher power.
3. Discuss with God, as you would with a friend, the need to be forgiven for mistakes you've made in previous relationships.
4. Learn about who God by completing a daily devotional through the Bible and attend a Bible-based church.
5. Develop an understanding of why you were created.
6. Begin to live your life purposefully.
7. Share your journey of self-discovery with other women.
8. Make a promise that you will not seek romantic love until you're ready to accept God's love. If you're in a romantic relationship, then vow to open your heart to fully loving yourself, so you can share this love with your partner.

~Life Scriptures~

"Whoever does not love does not know God, because God is love" (1 John 4:8).

"There is no fear in love. But perfect love drives out fear, because fear has to do with punishment. The one who fears is not made perfect in love" (1 John 4:18).

"Above all else, guard your heart, for it is the wellspring of life" (Proverbs 4:23).

"There are three things that amaze me—no, four things that I don't understand: how an eagle glides through the sky, how a snake slithers on a rock, how a ship navigates the ocean, how a man loves a woman" (Proverbs 30: 18-19, NLT).

"Many waters cannot quench love; rivers cannot wash it away. If one were to give all the wealth of his house for love, it would be utterly scorned" (Song of Solomon 8:7).

"Jesus replied: 'Love the Lord your God with all your heart and with all your soul and with all your mind.' This is the first and greatest commandment. And the second is like it: 'Love your neighbor as yourself" (Mathew 23:37-39).

"My lover is mine, and I am his" (Song of Solomon 2:16, NLT).

"Place me like a seal over your heart, like a seal on your arm; for love is as strong as death, its jealousy unyielding as the grave. It burns like blazing fire, like a mighty flame" (Song of Solomon 8:6).

"Greater love has no one than this, that he lay down his life for his friends" (John 15:13).

"Love is patient, love is kind. It does not envy, it does not boast, it is not proud. It does not dishonor others, it is not self-seeking, it is not easily angered, it keeps no record of wrongs. Love does not delight in evil but rejoices with the truth. It always protects, always trusts, always hopes, always perseveres. Love never fails. But where there are prophecies, they will cease; where there are tongues, they will be stilled; where there is knowledge, it will pass away" (1 Corinthians 13: 4-8).

"And now these three remain: faith, hope and love. But the greatest of these is love" (1 Corinthians 13:13).

"And over all these virtues put on love, which binds them all together in perfect unity" (Colossians 3:14).

"Above all, love each other deeply, because love covers over a multitude of sins" (1 Peter 4:8).

"This is how we know what love is: Jesus Christ laid down his life for us. And we ought to lay down our lives for our brothers and sisters" (1 John 3: 16).

"Place me like a seal over your heart, like a seal on your arm; for love is as strong as death, its jealousy unyielding as the grave. It burns like blazing fire, like a mighty flame" (Song of Solomon 8:16).

~Points to Ponder~

❖ Describe the word love.
❖ What Bible quotes discuss the topic of love? What do these scriptures indicate about God's love versus human love?

❖ Define in your own terms the word, wall. How does this world relate to the above poem?

❖ How "walls" around our heart block us from receiving or giving love?

❖ Define the word receive. Can you receive love with a walled heart? What tools can you use to help this process?

❖ Journal your plan to break down your emotional walls. As you journal think about this statement. Can an emotionally unavailable woman find, receive, and give love?

❖ Discuss these points to ponder among a group of other women.

CHAPTER 18

WILL I FIND A MATE?

There are moments in our life when we question whether God's plans are better than the plans, we created our self. We hear other people say that God is omnipotent, omniscient, and omnipresent, but what does that really mean? In some areas of our life, such as finances, maybe we understand these terms. We know that when our bank account dwindles God will provide the food we need. We think that God knows our human needs and somehow, they will be supplied. Yet, what about our social intimacy needs between us and a man? Sometimes it doesn't seem like God understands this need. Am I right? Waiting for God to supply us with our man/husband seems like a fairytale. God seemingly takes forever to show us those three "O's" when trying to find a mate.

When we are looking for Prince Charming to ride on his white horse and sweep us off our feet, God seems to have no part in bringing him into our life. Trusting God with our romantic lives is downright difficult. As a result, we take this matter into our own hands and leave God out of the equation. We lower God's capabilities to bring love. We don't believe God can bring the right man into our lives. I wish I could lecture you. I wish I could point the finger at you and not myself. Unfortunately, I can't. Finding a mate is an area in which I struggle too. I find myself doubting the power of God to find me love. I'm unsure if God can bring a husband. In certain areas of my life, God is the all-powerful, but in other areas I question His omnipotence. Can God do it? Will He fulfill His promise?

Many women have the same questions and doubt God will give them a lifetime-partner. During my singleness, I've had many nights where I cried asking God why everyone else was finding their mate except me. Now, I'm content with my singleness in my mid-30s, but the struggle has been a journey. I thought something was wrong with me. I had to be undesirable to marry. Flashbacks crossed my mind about my first relationship which ended in heartbreak. My mind recalled his cheating, lies, and words he uttered that I was the worse girlfriend he ever dated.

I recalled him calling me immature, unfit for marriage, and stating that I didn't complete a career path for my life. Sometimes I believed he was right. I didn't have it all together. Maybe my dreams were out my league. Insecurities stirred my mind. Could it be that I wasn't pretty, smart, stable, or godly? Pondering these negative thoughts brought crocodile tears. Not knowing what else to do, I decided to pray about my frustration. I released everything that burned in my heart. I knew God was listening, God is omnipresent. The sad truth was that I believed God was listening to my prayers, just not the part about me wanting a godly man. I assumed God didn't respond to me because He was thinking, "That's what you get for not listening when I told you not to date the first guy in the first place." Deep inside I yearned to know that everything was not my fault. I wanted to know that love would happen again.

I longed for the comfort from another person, a man. This future man would view me as a woman who is worthy of his love. At that point of my life I desired social intimacy beyond my parents or siblings. I was undergoing the psychosocial life stage of intimacy versus isolation. I didn't want only my family and close friends to love me. I wanted to be someone's wife. I wanted a man to see me as his queen, the mother of his children, his "rib," and a gift from God. Nevertheless, there was still no man in sight. What was God doing up there? Did He not hear my social desires?

Oh, what pitiful shame I would feel. Why was everyone else happily involved, engaged, or married? I even knew people who probably shouldn't be together but mended their relationship. Watching these couples made me wonder why my relationship never worked out. Why would a man treat me the way that he did? Only trash deserves to be put into a bag and thrown out. Was I waste? Was I garbage? I asked God to show me what was repulsive about me that caused this mistreatment. This way I could change those things and make myself better for the next man. I asked God to heal me from the resentment and heartache. I prayed for strength, direction, and patience. I didn't want this one circumstance to deter me from my marital destiny.

While asking God to transform me, I realized that He wanted the best for my life. He already had the best mate waiting to find me. It would be on God's timing, not mine. Even though my heart ached, there would come a time where I would rejoice. God knew I deserved better than what I had. Understand my sister that the man I once desired was destined to walk out of my life. If he stayed, I would have been distracted from following the plans of my destiny.

God did not allow me to continue with my past relationship(s) because he knew my husband could not be mediocre. My husband would have to be a man that edified me in every way. He would have to upgrade and not downgrade me. Therefore, I had to prepare for a man such as that.

Singleness was my calling for the time being in order to prepare me for my future mate. I wasn't ready to meet my man just yet. If I entered his life prematurely, before the EDD (Expected Date of Delivery) my unpreparedness would mess up the relationship.

During my preparation phase of singleness which I am still undergoing, I matured. The woman God called me to be continues to blossom. God saw the best in me. He continued to love me regardless of my flaws and imperfections. God was there through the thick and thin journeying along with me to the road of becoming a wife. This same circumstance may fit yours. Are you wondering where, when, and who will be your future lifelong partner?

~Will I find a Mate Challenge~

As you begin your journey to become a wife start with building your relationship with God. Discover who God created you to be. Recognizing the good and bad aspects of who you are is important. God will transform what's bad about you into good. The good will be transformed into greatness for you and your future relationship.

Never allow the thoughts or words of your ex(s) to define who you are. Don't allow other people to make you think that you're not what God says, a princess. God's word is the optimal truth. If the Bible says that you are worth dying for. Then so be it, you are. John 3:16 tells us that we were worthy to Him because He laid down His life for us. Believe that. Allow God's love to erase the negativity of your past relationships and transform you into the beautiful wife He always imagined you to be. In time, your mate will find you and you will find him.

~Life Scriptures~

"Ask and it will be given to you; seek and you will find; knock and the door will be opened to you. For everyone who asks receives; the one who seeks finds; and to the one who knocks, the door will be opened. "Which of you, if your son asks for bread, will give him a stone? Or if he asks for a fish, will give him a snake? If you, then, though you are evil, know how to give good gifts to your children, how much more will your Father in heaven give good gifts to those who ask him"" (Mathew 7:7-11).

"For I know the plans I have for you," declares the LORD, "plans to prosper you and not to harm you, plans to give you hope and a future"" (Jeremiah 29:11).

"Take delight in the LORD, and he will give you the desires of your heart" (Psalm 37:4).

"If any of you lacks wisdom, you should ask God, who gives generously to all without finding fault, and it will be given to you" (James 1:5).

"But those who hope in the LORD will renew their strength. They will soar on wings like eagles; they will run and not grow weary; they will walk and not be faint" (Isaiah 40:31).

"Every good and perfect gift is from above, coming down from the Father of the heavenly lights, who does not change like shifting shadows" (James 1:17).

~Points to Ponder~

- ❖ Why is it hard for you to trust God to bring your husband into your life?
- ❖ Are you seeking intimacy in all the wrong places or with the wrong people?
- ❖ Are you waiting for a man to see your value when God already does?
- ❖ Read John 3. Here you will see how much God loves you.
- ❖ Embrace God's love before you seek the embrace and love from someone else. God's love will prepare you for your mate. Without God's love, romantic love is difficult to function at its full potential.
- ❖ In addition to this book, I recommend that you read the "5 Love Languages by Dr. Chatman.
    1. What are your top two love languages?
    2. How too you give love?
    3. How do you receive love?

CHAPTER 19

WHO SHOULD I MARRY?

This book has journeyed along various topics we face as women, including finding our purpose and true love. In this chapter we will discuss easy tips to finding the right person for marriage. Sometimes meeting the right person is simpler than we think, but our lack of wisdom and/or patience causes dating to be overly complicated. Below are a few strategies that will aid you in discovering your match. The strategies given are the same that I use. Each strategy helps me discover my heart's desire about qualities I want in my future lifetime partner. Furthermore, these strategies assist me to set boundaries for my dating circle. This helps me to reduce the risks of having multiple failed relationships.

When setting boundaries for our dating circle, it causes us to eliminate incompatible daters. Why should you waste time on useless dates? Why settle for less than what you deserve? Why waste money on a person of no interest or can't see a future with? By setting boundaries for your dating pool it will prevent you from settling for less or waste precious time. Failing to set boundaries will more likely allow you to marry someone who is not equally yoked. Marrying someone undesired or unequally yoked places your marriage at a greater risk for divorce. Think about it. Would you be more willing to rectify marital differences with someone you truly desire to marry? Would you be willing to resolve differences with someone you married out of convenience? Your answers are probably respectively, yes and no.

Divorce rates are high. People no longer are staying together for better or worse. Statistics show that 50-70% of marriages result in divorce. My goal is to help you not fall into these statistical numbers. However, if you have experienced divorce, these tips can help you start over (considering you have asked for God's forgiveness and sought reconciliation with your partner).

It's all about being equally yoked.

Read 2 Corinthians 6:14-18. Ask yourself this question, "If one ox can pull a heavy load, can two oxen do a better job pulling that load?" The answer depends on whether each ox is going in the same direction. Are they traveling the same road, in the same direction, using the same tools? Or, are they traveling separate directions, using separate tools, and on different roads?

Based on the direction they are going you'll get a final answer. If the oxen are in sync going the same direction, then they will be able to pull the load. However, if traveling separate ways, they cannot.

We can relate this to relationships. A couple in sync can pull the weight of their relationship but, a couple not in sync cannot. You see, the two persons pulling the weight must be equally compatible or "yoked." A couple being equally yoked goes beyond having the same religion or denominational beliefs. Being equally yoked supersedes these ideals and goes to the heart of the matter. What direction are you both moving? How do both of your lives sync? Do you have similar goals, beliefs, spiritual visions, and a willingness to work together to accomplish your life goals?

Let's go a little deeper. A yoke is defined as a crosspiece that's usually wooden and is placed around the necks of two oxen. This crosspiece binds the two by the neck and forces them to walk in the same direction. Using the yoke in the olden days was an essential tool for plowing farmland. Farmers preferred to use more than one ox to complete daily duties because it was more efficient. Two oxen created increased strength and maximized the ability to perform the strenuous task. However, using the two animals without placing a yoke on them made the job extremely difficult. Without the yoke to bind the oxen together they would walk in separate directions and incomplete the tasks.

Picture this…

A farmer ties two oxen with separate ropes to his plow. The farmer's task is to plow the land before sunset. As the farmer begins to plow, one ox decides to walk towards the left and the other walks to the right. Each ox wants to walk a different path to reach something different in the horizon. Maybe one ox sees a green field over a hill and the other wants to rest by a tree. Both want different things and must go different ways. The further each ox drifts away from the other, the further away they drift from the task to plow the land. Tension on the ropes will increase and pull it apart. What do you think will happen?

The tension will rise, the strings will loosen, and eventually the ropes will break. Their task to plow the land before sunset will be left unfinished. The land will be left in ruins. As a result, the farmer must stop in his tasks, grab the two oxen, and figure out a way to bind them back together. He must bind them so they will walk together on the same path to accomplish the plowing. This is where the yoke comes into play. Binding the oxen with the yoke forces them to move in the same direction. Even if one ox decides to go left and the other right, they won't be able to. They will have to agree to go in one direction, completing the plowing together, or not at all.

Get the picture? Being equally yoked in our relationship has to do with two people choosing to walk together in the same direction of life, seeking to accomplish similar tasks. If a couple has a separate visions and desires, then they will drift separate ways. The rope of love that binds them will loosen and break. They will drift apart, leaving tasks undone, and plans ruined. This is not to say that each person will be just like the other. Rather, the couple will have similar visions, goals, beliefs, and ideas. They will be yoked together with a strong bond that will allow them to accomplish their God-given tasks. In other words, God will be their farmer and He will yoke them together with His guided word. This way they will stick together to accomplish the tasks God gave them. Understanding the need to be equally yoked is great and dandy, but how do you find your "ox"?

Strategy #1- Prioritize.

The first strategy is organizing your life. You must get to a place in life where your priorities are correct. God must be your priority. It makes no sense to worry about getting married if you lack a relationship with the One who created marriage. As discussed in chapter 20, marriage is not about physical attraction or sex. Marriage is about partnership and divine love. Understanding the essence of marriage and the God who instituted it, is a priority! Marriage has a deeper concept than what most people believe. It was instituted by God as a spiritual depiction of God's love towards His creation (Ephesians 5). Marriage also serves as a ministry of encouragement between lifelong lovers. If you lack an understanding of God, the marriage institutor, then you will lack an understanding of marriage. Thus, you will lack tools to sustain a marriage. Only by having a relationship with God first, can you become equipped to sustain a happy marriage.

While prioritizing your life you also should understand your past and close its chapter. What choices did you make? How has your past affected your life? Whatever anger, un-forgiveness, negative circumstances, or ungodly habits you possessed must be addressed. This way healing can begin. Without healing from your past, you can't close those chapters and open a new one. As a result, you won't be able to find true love. Why? Number one, you won't be ready to give or receive love. Number two, resentment, hostility, and bad habits from your past will be carried into your future. You'll be prone to destroy your relationship.

For example, take this fictional story of a man and woman. Neither of them dealt with their past or built a relationship with their creator while single. They met each other at a local bar one summer. She was gorgeous and he smelled good, so they began talking about love, sex, and money. After that night they continued seeing each other and became exclusive. During their dating period several issues of their past were brought up in conversation. She expressed to him that she never experienced a solid relationship. He expressed that he never had a father in his life. She told him that she had difficulty trusting a man and it often carried into the way she acted in her relationships. Oftentimes she would find herself thinking about her past and became easily angered. Sometimes she'd feel the need to lash her anger out on her boyfriends. She never healed from her past issues and still resented her past choices. There was still a secret in the air why her relationships always failed, but she never revealed that to anyone.

The boyfriend believed that things would get better if he proved how much he loved her. He figured that he had issues in his past as well, so what was the worry? His father was never there, and his mother was a drug addict. Over the years, he developed the mindset that no one would be able to connect closely to his heart because he didn't want to get hurt. Although it didn't seem like it to his new woman, he built emotional walls that she'd never be able to break. He allowed people to come into his life, but not into his heart. He could love, but not to the point of sacrificial, unconditional love.

Neither he nor his girlfriend resolve their past issues. Thus, the issues of their past were brought into their future marriage. After the romance and sex dwindled, past issues began surfacing. The woman often lashed out at the slightest mistake he made. The husband would push himself away from her heart after each lashing. He refused to open and discuss the hurt her lashings caused. Eventually their marriage landed between a rock and a hard place. They didn't know how to begin dealing with their issues. Instead of owning up to the past and seeking counseling, the two called it quits. They felt that things changed. However, things were always that way. They just chose to ignore the issues of their past from the beginning of their relationship. Neither of them took adequate time during their singleness to reevaluate their lives.

Neither person took time out for self-discovery, healing, and finding their life's purpose. Consequently, as they entered a new chapter of life, the old chapters followed. Do you understand the point of closing the chapters of your past before getting into a relationship? Without doing this you cannot sustain a happy marriage. Your old life will destroy your new life. You must let go of the old to grab the new. To do this you have to have a relationship with your creator. Below is a list of how to prioritize your life to prepare for marriage:

❖ Learning about God is your priority.
❖ Discovering who you are is second priority.
❖ Dealing with your past is additional to your second priority.
❖ Learning the purpose of marriage is third.
❖ Fourth priority is learning what makes a woman a wife.
❖ Fifth priority is discovering what makes a man a husband.
❖ Discovering your heart's desire for marriage is sixth.

Strategy#2 - Self-discovery.

The second strategy after prioritizing your life is to take a journey of self-discovery. You'll learn why you were created, what's a life purpose, and why God wants to spiritually commune with you. The best thing about taking this self-discovery journey is getting to learn the true meaning of love. Read John 3:16. Learning what love consists of is critical in developing a solid relationship with a future mate. The purpose of a romantic relationship is to display God's supernatural love. The more we understand God's love, the more we understand what romantic love is about.

As a woman begins to understand the love her Creator has given towards her, laying down His life, her heart will become encircled with love. That woman will understand her love potential and desire to share that love with others. Why is this important? Your relationship with Christ serves as an example of your future love relationship with your mate. If you lack a relationship with your Creator, you will lack one with your mate. An unhappy relationship with the One who created you, will lead to an unhappy relationship with a man. How can you love someone else if you don't love yourself? How can you love yourself if you don't love the One who created you?

Love comes from our creator. God is the source of love. God is the one who can teach us how to love. If you don't possess God's sacrificial love, then you can't love unconditionally. Loving unconditionally is the key to making a marriage work. Therefore, after prioritizing your life, the next strategy is to discover who you are. Let's take a quick look at the significance of marital love. "My people are being destroyed because they don't know me..." (Hosea 4:6, NLT).

Strategy#3 - Divine guidance

Strategy number three involves God guiding (directing) your thoughts to discover your heart's desire for a future mate. Take it from me, this step takes longer than you may think. It requires patience. Seeking God's opinion on what type of mate you should marry cannot be done overnight. This process involves surrendering to God's idea of an ideal mate. Many of us tell God what we desire in a man, leading us to choose a man without guidance. Following our own desires can lead to disaster but, following God's wisdom leads to marital bliss. The following mini steps should be completed to master the third strategy:

1) Pray for guidance concerning which qualities your match should have. Read scriptures that provide wisdom about marriage. Review the books of Proverbs, Song of Solomon, and Ephesians.
2) Develop your traits into that of a woman who can become a wife.
3) Cultivate your character to meet the needs of your future husband. Ask God to shape your personality to fit the needs of your future mate.
4) Pray for God to help your future mate develop his character to meet your needs.
5) Eliminate dating candidates who don't line up to God's standards.

Following each mini step will guide you. At God's perfect timing you will meet "Mr. made for you." When you meet him, there is one last concept to keep in mind.

Strategy#4 Prepare to be a wife

Strategy number four is where you will evolve into a single woman prepared to be a wife. Although we like to plan our wedding day, it's more important to plan our marriage. Keep in mind that marriage is not a one-time event where we wear a white dress. That is called a wedding. So many of us confuse the idea of marriage with a wedding day. Many engaged couples spend thousands of hours on details of their wedding. However, they do not work on the details of their marriage, leaving them unprepared for the journey. This is where the last strategy takes place. Once strategy three is completed and you've met your future spouse, it's time to prepare for your lifelong commitment. Do not wait until after the wedding. Your pre-marital/singleness stage is the time to get this out the way. While you are exclusively dating you should address pertinent issues like:

- ❖ How many children do you want?
- ❖ How will finances be handled?
- ❖ What roles will we both play?
- ❖ What are your spiritual beliefs?
- ❖ What are your ideals for family functioning?
- ❖ What are each person's ideas on sexuality?

These types of questions and those important to you, should be answered while courting. Dating is not time to be wasted on infatuation. At the same time, it's not a time to brutally interrogate each other. It's a time to grow beyond your physical attractions. It's a time to learn about the person you're going to share your life. Get the hard questions out the way so that you can enjoy marriage. Discuss,

- ❖ Finance
- ❖ Children
- ❖ Residence
- ❖ Love
- ❖ Sex
- ❖ Spirituality

These are critical during the engagement. I suggest you receive the help from a Christian marriage counselor.

I have not covered every detail how to find your perfect husband. That would take an entire book. This chapter was written to provide you with a foundation on how to date. The four strategies will assist you on your journey from singleness to marriage. They can help you determine what type of man is equally compatible, yoked. There are books dedicated to this topic and can be found in your local bookstore. Lastly, the greatest guidance can be found in the Bible and through prayer/meditation.

~Who Should I Marry Challenge~

My challenge to you is recognize that you deserve the best, even your married life. God cares about who you marry, when you will marry, why you will marry, and your happiness. He does not desire for you to settle for less. He wants you to be equally yoked. As you use the strategies provided, keep in mind that each strategy is not be useful without strategy number one!

~Life Scriptures~

"If you believe, you will receive whatever you ask for in prayer" (Matthew 21:22).

"Promise me, O women of Jerusalem, not to awaken love until the time is right" (Song of Solomon 8:4).

"For God so loved the world that he gave his one and only Son, that whoever believes in him shall not perish but have eternal life. For God did not send his Son into the world to condemn the world, but to save the world through him. Whoever believes in him is not condemned, but whoever does not believe stands condemned already because he has not believed in the name of God's one and only Son" (John 3:16-18).

"Ask and it will be given to you; seek and you will find; knock and the door will be opened to you. For everyone who asks receives; the one who seeks finds; and to the one who knocks, the door will be opened. "Which of you, if your son asks for bread, will give him a stone? Or if he asks for a fish, will give him a snake? If you, then, though you are evil, know how to give good gifts to your children, how much more will your Father in heaven give good gifts to those who ask him?" (Matthew 7:7-11).

"My lover is mine, and I am his" (Song of Solomon 2:16, NLT).

~Points to Ponder~

❖ In your own words explain the four strategies to discover your ideal mate.
❖ What strategy is the most important? Explain.
❖ In your note pad write your journey of love and self-discovery.
❖ Where does love begin?
❖ How is your love obtained and given to others?
❖ Discuss within a group why many women marry the wrong person.
❖ How can we avoid marrying someone who isn't equally yoked?

❖ List your heart's desire for your mate and non-negotiable qualities. While dating, these qualities are your boundaries.

CHAPTER 20

DO I WANT SEX OR MARRIAGE?

"I want a husband. Lord, just give me a man. I don't care which man. Any man will do! My biological clock is ticking." Does this sound like something you find yourself saying? I have shocking news, statements like this usually come from women who desire someone else to make them happy. This type of attitude displays that we have a lack of understanding about marriage. Contrary to popular belief, there is a difference between having a man and a husband. You may be confused about what I mean. Let me explain. A husband requires more than physical companionship or sex. The responsibility of being a wife is enormous. It should never be taken lightly. If you simply desire life-long legal sex or someone to make you happy, you'll find that your marriage will end or be unhappy.

Proverbs 31:10-12 reads, "A wife of noble character who can find? She is worth far more than rubies. Her husband has full confidence in her and lacks nothing of value. She brings him good, not harm, all the days of her life." The rest of this chapter will expound on this passage so that you can put it into practical use. Read Proverbs 31.

A wife is a woman of virtue.

When God formed you in your mother's womb, God dreamed of you being born as a precious jewel. He desired for you to grow in virtue, moral excellence. God dreamed of you becoming a woman who had characteristics of integrity and moral standing. He wants you to be a woman who knows her worth and waits for love at the right time. God wants you to understand that you were expensive in value because He bought you with a high price— His life. You are priceless, God's precious jewel. You are not just any type of woman. You should not live your life just any type of way.

As a woman of moral value, you cannot act like a lady who is associated with street living. In others, you can't be ratchet and ghetto sis which is a woman who lacks understanding of her value and squanders her jewels. People, especially your future husband, should be able to tell the difference between you and, as we say, a "scallywag." A scallywag squanders her love, time, affection, and sexual gifts with many men. She lacks understanding of her worth and life's purpose. However, God does not want that lifestyle for you or any woman. He doesn't want us to make a lifestyle out of squandering our value.

God desires us not to be women of promiscuity, rather women filled with worth. By God's love and principles, we should treat our bodies with respect. If we once lacked an understanding about our value, we can change our mindsets. We can love ourselves the way God intended. We were not created to be ordinary. We are women created for purpose and to serve a special purpose in marriage. There should be something deep within us that stands above the crowd. I like how DJ Khalid sings it, "You stick out of the crowd, baby it's a no brainer." Don't settle to be just any type of woman. Be a woman that has a special gift to give the world and her future man.

If you don't stand above other women can you attract a man to marry you? I think most men will tell you that if a woman does not stand out in his mind there will be nothing special about her. She'll be like all the other women he's met. Why would he choose to marry you when you're just like every other woman he's had? What are you doing to separate yourself and character? What is it about you that would cause him to say that you're special? Or, are you okay with being just like Kesha and Tanisha? Are you a woman of value?

In order to be special, you may not agree, you must place God at the center of your life so His beauty can shine through your soul. Remember we talked about allowing God to erase your shameful past, change your present, and create the best future for you? Coming to terms with these will allow you to learn how to be a woman that is set apart. A lot of us think that a pretty face and good sex will set us apart. For example, The Kardashians. What happens? Eventually beauty and booty wear off. The once mesmerizing effects wears off. There are many pretty women that come a dime a dozen. You cannot think that your outward beauty will maintain a marriage.

Another huge misconception is that sex holds a marriage together. Aren't there women who claim to be the best at this? Then, why would he stay with you for the rest of his life? There must be something that makes a woman stand out from the rest. So, what is it that will make you special? It's your virtuousness, morals, love, compassion, forgiveness, soul glow, patience, purpose, and relationship with your creator. It's also your understanding of your worth. Understanding these things will cause a man to look beyond your exterior to see your interior beauty. He will not view you as just a sexual object, rather, a gift that he cherishes. However, you must create that image through your character. Let him learn to caresses your mind, emotions, and spirit, caressing your body.

Unlike all the other women he's been with, he will not just understand the way your body works sexually. He'll understand your thoughts, emotions, and spiritual patterns. If you allow a man to grasp the interior aspect of you, he will learn the essence of who you are. He can recognize your marital potential and purpose in his life. Having virtue is important to become a wife.

A wife knows her sexual worth.

Understanding your sexual worth is essential before becoming married. Without recognizing that sex isn't just sex, you can make mistakes and experience heartache. To avoid making wrong decisions and keep emotional availability, you must know your sexual worth. From your kisses to caresses, they are valuable. They should be bought with a price—the price of commitment. You don't want a man to only know your lips and not who you are. Any woman can kiss a man. However, you are not just any woman. Do something different. Most women don't value their body, do the opposite. If a guy gets in your underwear before marriage, you become panties to him. He loses his love. Read 2 Samuel 13 about Tamar and Absalom. Did you see how Absalom changed?

I'm not saying that men are the prize. I am saying that most men think differently from us. We should learn to protect our hearts. Yes, a lot of people have sex before marriage and what do they say? They say that after marriage the sex becomes old and commonplace. Like, what? Really? So, if we give it up all the time prior to marriage, its likely that after marriage we slow down? Isn't that crazy? The truth is that a lot of couples struggle with sexual enjoyment after marriage. Don't you think it's because of something we do wrong during the process?

Most men say that not having sex before marriage would not make them choose not to marry the women they love. However, when a man is not willing to wait, more than likely his love is not genuine, or godly. Majority of men will not buy the cow when they're getting the milk free! When you meet a man, discuss your sexual values. Discuss boundaries. Can you handle kissing and not take it further? Will you be inclined to sleep with him if you constantly kiss? You must know your mind and body. Do what is needed to prevent falling into unnecessary traps. Be upfront. If a man desires you, he will respect the boundaries and remain in the relationship. If not, you know what his motives were.

Display your worth through your sexual actions. If you claim to be different, then act different. Don't claim to be virtuous but, be a freak in the sheets when he's not your husband. If you do, he may begin to take you as a joke or question your character.

A wife watches her mouth.

So many women do not understand the importance of the words they speak. Many times, we speak negative and degrading things to the men in our life. We fail to realize that every time a negative word flows out our mouth into the ear of our man, he slowly dies at loving us. Men are looking for you to build them up, not put them down. Learning when and when not to speak your mind is crucial in maintaining a good marriage.

Don't claim to be a virtuous woman and then cuss him out. That makes no sense to his mind. Each time you cuss him out, he will view you as a woman of less value. You may be thinking, what about when he makes me angry or does something stupid? Don't I have the right to cuss him out? Do that if you want but, know that in his mind you're a laughing matter. Men do not respond the way we think they should. R.C. Blakes is a great teacher about how men think, as well as Steve Harvey. I suggest that you read their books. What would make a bigger impact is a woman who knows what to say, how to say it, and when to say it. Sis trust me, I know how difficult this is. A woman of virtue asks God to hold her tongue, so she won't lash out of anger and say things she regrets later to her spouse. Men are fragile inside and your words have power!

It's not necessary to say everything or have the last word. In order to stand out, you must learn to calm down. Cussing, screaming, and yelling only shows you have not matured to handle stress. It shows childlike behavior and inadequate vocabulary. It shows that you are no different from other women. Most women will cuss out a man, but if you remain calm, he will be amazed! Plus, you'll have less stress and if he's truly that bad, then don't marry him. Don't let a man stress you out! The most powerful thing to do is pray, not cuss. Cussing will not change a situation or a man, but prayer will!

Remember, "Love is patient, love is kind. It does not boast; it is not proud. It is not rude, it is not self-seeking, it is not easily angered, it keeps no record of wrongs. Love does not delight in evil but rejoices with the truth. It always protects, always trusts, always hopes, always perseveres. Love never fails" (1 Corinthians 13:4-8). Your love needs to be a haven for your man, so does your mouth. When he's getting a verbal beating at work, your mouth should be soothing to his inner hurts. Men do have feelings and if he can't get positive feedback from you, he'll find it somewhere else. Usually, it's in the arms of another woman who's learned the trick of positivity.

Be careful what you speak. You may cause your own destruction. Instead of cussing, inform him what is bothering you. Tell him how it affects you. Talk to him about your expectations. If he can't develop into someone better, you may want to think about another option before marrying him. If you are married, then you should positively push him and pray for him. Do not speak negatively to your man/husband.

A wife knows her purpose.

You were destined with purpose. Before you are married begin walking in this purpose. God designed singleness as time to find your niche. Finding your niche gives you a sense of purpose and finances. Women were not created to be lazy. We can be entrepreneurs. As Cardi B says, "let's get this shhmoney." Read Proverbs 31. "She sets about her work vigorously; her arms are strong for her tasks. She sees that her trading is profitable, and her lamp does not go out at night" (Proverbs 31:17-18).

Women were designed to be helpmeets. Your husband may be the provider for the home, but the bread winner maybe you. He may be in a field where his salary cannot meet all the family's needs, so how will the needs be met? You! Your God-given talents will help. Your talents and money can be used as assets. For example, your income can pay off debt. Your talents are important. Proverbs 31 clearly states that a wife knows how to perform household chores too. She must be prepared to take care of her home. So, are you capable to prepare meals? Are you able to provide a hospitable environment? If not, you can begin learning basic home economics.

In your singleness get into the routine of completing household chores so it will not be a chore once married. It will be part of your character. Keep your home in organized. Learn cooking techniques, review cooking books, and try new recipes. Take a home economics course or marriage preparedness retreat. Why wait until you are married and have the difficulty of learning the basics? Become a well-rounded woman. Whether working in corporate or at home your most important job is your family. They are the biggest reflection of who you are.

A wife is trustworthy.

Marriage is not easy. Adding untrustworthiness only complicates matters. Marriage needs each partner to be faithful to God and then to each other. It's a sacred union between a man, woman, and their creator. The question is, are you a trustworthy woman? Trust goes beyond abstaining from sexual relations with someone outside of your marriage. When your husband trusts you, it means that he has full confidence in you! You know, how Barack trusts Michelle! That type of full confidence. The confidence where your husband can rely on you to do the right thing for the right reason. "Her husband has full confidence in her and lacks nothing of value" (Proverbs 31:11).

Your husband should have confidence that you'll provide for him and your family's basic needs. Your home should be a place of peace, rest, comfort, and encouragement. Most of all he should be able to trust you with his heart and intimate secrets. You should not share intimate things about your husband to your girlfriends, or family. You don't know what is in the minds of other people. You do not know their ulterior motives. You may be giving people an edge on how to separate your marriage. Your girlfriends may even have an eye for your man. Use wisdom when discussing your relationship to others. Don't allow anyone to destroy your covenant. Be trustworthy.

A wife prospers her husband.

"Her husband is respected at the city gate, where he takes his seat among the elders of the land" (Proverbs 31:23). As a woman of worth you can prosper your husband. As the saying goes, behind every good man is a great woman! Look at the first ladies of the United States. They are perfect examples how a woman prospers her husband. Just as God gave you a niche, God has given one to your husband. As his wife, you should support him reaching his God-given goals. You are his backbone. You can help direct and move him towards his destiny through wise encouragement. This requires a woman who knows her purpose, talents, and worth.

Do not be a hindrance to your man. Do not tear him down verbally, emotionally, spiritually, or sexually. What do I mean? I mean your words and actions should build his confidence. Your actions should reassure his purpose. Treat him the way you want him to treat you! Make him feel that he is the best thing since sliced bread, ladies even when you know he isn't. Understand that through prayer, he can change for the better. Don't tear him down financially by overspending and bringing on debt. Don't withhold finances either. Give to him just as he gives to you. Be careful and spend wisely on the necessities.

Don't spiritually abuse him by speaking death or negative things about him into his life. Don't deprive him of encouraging words. Don't allow him to get off track when it comes to serving God. Remember the ultimate goal is to help your spouse journey to heaven. Don't pick physical fights with your husband. If you've been in abusive relationships, you must seek help to deal with underlying issues and learn to cope in stressful situations. Don't throw pots and pans at him. Learn appropriate ways to deal with tough times and your anger, like deep breathing. I will say this, please make sure you marry someone who God sees fit for your life. Then your chances of reverting to abusive behaviors will be reduced. Your husband should be able to look at your life and desire to become a better man.

"The wise woman builds her house, but with her own hands the foolish one tears hers down" (Proverbs 14:1). More importantly, in a marriage we are to go to God about everything! As women, we love to voice everything upfront. However, this is not always effective. Your husband doesn't need to hear you voice his faults and flaws all the time. Rather, he needs to hear you voice his strengths. The faults that you see in him should be taken to God in prayer. Then, at the right time you can explain to your mate what needs to be a changed to better the relationship. Don't nag him because he will start to resent you. Again, men are different! They don't want a nagging wife. "Better to live on a corner of the roof than share a house with a quarrelsome wife" (Proverbs 21:9). You are called to be a blessing, not a curse. Prosper your man.

Heather Lindsey is a great role model for single and married women. She gives hardcore advice on how to become better women prior to and after marriage. I suggest checking out her ministry.

A wife knows her ultimate purpose.

Ultimately, you should enrich your husband's life and assist him in his journey to heaven. During your singleness prepare for marriage. Marriage is not a joke and it's not about looking pretty or sex. Marriage is a lifetime work of helping your spouse and family become all that they can be.

~Do I want Sex or Marriage Challenge~

My challenge to you is to prepare for marital success. Learn the ins and outs of marriage. Learn the role a wife and that of a husband. Before you become married understand your purpose and sexual.

~Life Scripture~

"A wife of noble character who can find? She is worth far more than rubies. Her husband has full confidence in her and lacks nothing of value. She brings him good, not harm, all the days of her life. She selects wool and flax and works with eager hands" (Proverbs 31:10-13).

"The tongue has the power of life and death, and those who love it will eat its fruit" (Proverbs 18:21).

"Many women do noble things, but you surpass them all. Charm is deceptive, and beauty is fleeting; but a woman who fears the LORD is to be praised. Honor her for all that her hands have done, and let her works bring her praise at the city gate" (Proverbs 31:29-31).

"Then Amnon hated her with intense hatred. In fact, he hated her more than he had loved her. Amnon said to her, "Get up and get out! No! she said to him. Sending me away would be a greater wrong than what you have already done to me" (2 Samuel 13:15-16).

~Points to Ponder~

❖ In your own terms define the word wife?

❖ How have you prepared for marriage?

❖ What are your sexual boundaries?

❖ Which talents do you possess that can be used as a career purpose?

❖ Take the Myers-Briggs test to find out your personality type and career niche.

❖ What domestic skills do you have to enhance your marriage?

❖ Challenge yourself by taking a home economics course.

❖ What did you learn reading Proverbs 31, Proverbs 7, and 2 Samuel 13?

- ❖ Contrast the woman from Proverbs 31 to that of Proverbs 7.
- ❖ How can you hinder or prosper your marriage?
- ❖ In your note pad list basic characteristics a woman should have to maintain a happy marriage.
- ❖ Discuss within a group this chapter's main point.

CHAPTER 21

ROLE PLAY

Many women are thrilled with the idea of getting married, something they look forward to accomplishing. During the journey of becoming married, they tend to acquaint themselves with wedding plans, but never the meaning and purpose of being a wife. To think past the wedding day to the actual marriage is farfetched. As a result, too many women have a poor understanding about marriage and the role of a wife.

Today women are getting married without any idea how their roles serve as a divine purpose within their marriage. Marriage is more than a fantasy world. It requires two people who understand their purpose of being together. It's the combining of two lives, souls, minds, and hearts. "The man said, "This is now bone of my bones and flesh of my flesh; she shall be called 'woman,' for she was taken out of man." That is why a man leaves his father and mother and is united to his wife, and they become one flesh" (Genesis 2:23-24).

Marriage is deeper than its physical union, it's the union of two souls. When the two joins together, they form one union, empowered to change their surroundings. Depending on how each partner understands their marital role, their marriage will either be empowered or disempowered. Therefore, women must understand the significance of their marital role.

A wife's role.

The wife is called to be the side rib, backbone, support to her husband and family. She plays a major role in congealing the family together. "The Lord God said, "It is not good for man to be alone. I will make a helper suitable for him"" (Genesis 2:18). We see here that Eve was created as Adam's helpmeet, the very one that stuck by his side. Eve stood beside Adam giving him companionship, comfort, love, and assistance. God didn't make just any old thing for Adam. He designed a special WOMAN. From Adam's own rib, a mate was made suitable just for him. Genesis 2:23 says, "The man said, "This is now bone of my bones and flesh of my flesh; she shall be called 'woman,' for she was taken out of man."

What was significant about the creation of Eve? Even though Adam had a relationship with His Creator, there was a longing for human connection. Did God satisfy all of Adam's needs? The answer is, yes. However, God created a place in Adam's heart that desired someone else to share in his life adventure. Adam wasn't designed to live his life alone. So, God made Eve. As people say, she was the crowning act of all creation. She was the cherry on top of the ice cream, so to speak.

After Eve was created Adam no longer pined after companionship. He had it 24/7. In Genesis 1 and 2, he found his missing piece. There she'd walk alongside him, completing him for the rest of his life. I can imagine that everywhere Eve went, Adam followed suit. He probably couldn't get enough of her. The same for Eve, I imagine that everywhere Adam went she followed along. Even when she stood at the tree of the forbidden fruit, Adam stood beside her. He didn't leave her side. This should have been the only time he left her. Here is something to consider. Genesis 3 says that they both ate the forbidden fruit, they were beside each other. She never left his side and he doesn't leave hers. Through good and bad times, she was always right there. This displays the role of a wife. She is to stand by her husband through the good and bad, giving him companionship along the way.

Women exemplify stick-to-itiveness.

That's not a wife's only role, however. She is to be a jewel of wisdom for her family. She teaches her family and husband to appreciate feminine-like qualities, meekness, serenity, laughter, beauty, and wisdom. These are beatitudes of Christ (read Mathew 5) and she should display these characteristics. Her feminine-like qualities help her family learn what God is like. They learn His patience, love, and compassion from the wife. These factors are important because she inspires them to learn about God, where they become more prone to develop a personal relationship with Him.

Understand that your femininity plays a divine role in your marriage by displaying God's compassionate love.

Marriage displays God's love for His people and His plan brings them back into having a relationship with Him. This concept is so significant that the Bible reiterates it several times. Read Ephesians 5:22-33. God instituted marriage from the beginning of the world to display His love for His creation. Being omniscient, He knew the first marriage with Adam and Eve would fail to represent this love correctly. So, He sacrificed himself for them and us.

Reviewing Ephesians 5:22, it becomes clear that what Jesus did by sacrificing Himself is to be what our husbands do. Our husbands display Jesus and we display the church.

Through this example, husbands should be willing to commit the same sacrifice for love. In turn, as the wife, we should praise our man for the sacrifices he's willing to make to save our lives from danger, just like we should praise Jesus for sacrificing His life to save us.

Women represent the church. The church is God's people who praise, worship, and love Him. Taking this into consideration, we can conclude that the wife is the edifier of her husband. She empowers him by edifying him with encouraging words and acts. In addition, she also edifies and encourages each family member. The woman has something special about her. She has a womb, and the ability to bring forth life and purpose. She can use what she is impregnated with to give life to her family. Impregnated with life means her feminine qualities make her capable to empower each family member to become all that they can be.

She is known as a birthing pillar. Not just physically but, emotionally and spiritually. She awakens the soul with her feminine touch. Think of a woman who was a great mother and wife. What did she do to deserve this title? More than likely she cultivated the best assets in every member of her household. Like the virtuous woman in Proverbs 31, she took care of the family by empowering their abilities, preparing meals to eat, maintaining a clean environment, assisting financially, and unconditionally loving her family. This is a significant role. Although men can have similar qualities, they aren't designed to be fully equipped with these abilities. For instance, he isn't a woman, whereas he can bring forth life.

Ephesians.

The wife is called to submit to Christ's plan for her husband. What do I mean? As we read in Ephesians, the church submits to God's plans for their life. They are to trust that God loves them enough to do what is best for them. The church is to believe that God will never do something to hurt them or misguide them. As we spoke about earlier, the church represents the woman and Jesus represents the man. This means that the wife is to submit, place her full trust, in her husband. She is to trust that the decisions he makes are out for her best interest and not to harm her. This does not mean that she is mindless woman; instead she's in-tune with God as she allows Him to lead through the life of her man. She willingly allows her husband to take on his

God-given role as the leader of the home. Therefore, you have to marry the right type of man. Otherwise, you will get a poor leader, or someone not led by God. You must make a choice to marry someone that you will choose to lead your home and submit. You have the power to choose and choose wisely.

When your husband is in Christ, you don't have anything to fear about him leading the home. He will make decisions based on the love he has for God and for you. Ephesians 5 tells us that the husband's decisions are to be founded by unconditional love and seeking godly wisdom. However, if the decisions of your man are not founded in God, it is your duty to find these answers through prayer. Don't get it twisted, you are a leader in the home, but you lead in a different way—a feminine way. He leads in masculine demeanor. Neither way is more significant than the other. Just as much as you need him to lead and provide, your husband will need you for comfort, support, and wisdom. Remember that saying, "Behind every GOOD man is a GREAT woman."

Look at the first ladies of our nation. They are strong women and yet they are submissive. They allow themselves to be used to empower their husbands and family into success. At the same time, these women were strong leaders. They must have understood the concepts stated in Proverbs 31.

The wife is a vital part of the family, the holding piece known as the rib. Think of her like we do of a spinal cord that holds the body together. She is critical in assisting the body to get to its destination. Even if the brain (let's say the brain is a man, figuratively speaking) signals to the body to walk, the body cannot go anywhere without a spine. It would just flop on the ground. The brain needs the spinal cord, without it can't move. The woman is also the missing rib that extends from the spinal cord to protect the vital organ. She is what protects the inner man. She protects him from emotional and mental harm. How you wonder is by edifying him and speaking positively into his life. She also knows his weak spots but, will refuse to tell anyone else. She is his haven.

Role of submission.

As a Christian woman, you must understand your husband's role. As discussed, his role is to exemplify Christ. Therefore, as a man gives his life for you and the family, you are to submit to what God does through him. It is not an act of belittlement. If a woman is being belittled, then she is being abused. Being abused is different from being submissive. Too many women have these two terms confused because they were taught wrong or experienced bad relationships. Just because a man from your past relationships misused the term doesn't justify you disregarding God's natural concept for marriage. If you reject this concept, you will lose out on being feminine and a man's masculinity.

Never think that abuse is submissiveness.

Submission to your husband is a display of appreciation for his life-leading qualities. The husband should treat you like royalty. Thus, as a gift to his chivalry, you find ways to reward him. One of the best ways is allowing him to carry out his God-given purpose of being a leader. Allow your husband to lead the family. He wants to provide, cherish, and protect you. Let him do it. This is a choice for you to make. You are not forced to do it; it's your willingness to submit to your husband's leadership. It shows him that you trust in his abilities, love, and respect him. Why is that hard to do? If you are thinking because all men are dogs, that's the wrong concept. The truth is you dated men who were dogs. That's a choice you made. Don't make your good man pay for that. You'll be sorry if you decide to take on two roles in the marriage. You will end up finding yourself single again.

Too many women fail to submit to their great husbands and seek to overpower them. It's almost like the feminist movement created a movement where women are trying to overpower men instead of seeking to be equal to them. We have gone from wanting a place in life to abolishing the need for men. We overdid the entire concept and now everyone's role has been messed up.

We became cursed because of our fore-parents bit into the forbidden fruit. Genesis 3:16 states, "To the woman he said, "I will make your pains in childbearing very severe; with painful labor you will give birth to children. Your desire will be for your husband, and he will rule over you.'" We've been cursed ever since. When women try to overpower men in marriage, we take ourselves back to the Garden of Eden. Often our results are divorce, or an unhappy marriage. If we don't get divorced or become unhappy, the other result is our man becoming a complete wuss. You'd make him powerless and his role of leadership insignificant. He'll no longer feel masculine. He won't know how to provide or lead his family anymore. The family will be turned upside down and become dysfunctional.

What about the dark side of being submissive? A woman who marries an abusive man is coerced to heed to the man's every way of doing things.

Understand that God said to submit to a godly man, not an abusive one. As I said before, make sure you marry someone who understands the depth of his role as a husband. When you marry the man God leads you to, abuse more than likely, will not be an issue in your marriage. Be careful in who you choose to share the rest of your life with. Don't lose out on the beauty of God's marital plan.

Role of a Super-woman.

A woman is called to be who God has desired for her to be. If God has given her a career purpose and a desire to make a difference in the world, then her career is a part of who she is. If God has given a woman the career of being a homemaker, which is a part of whom she is. God may even call her to be a superwoman. These women are equipped by God to handle the duties of working in the corporate world, being a virtuous wife, and a nurturing mother. Not everyone woman can handle this task. Find out your God-given capabilities first. Prioritize your family life accordingly. Remember, your purpose as the wife and mother.

What a woman must keep in mind is that whatever career she has, it is a part of who she is. The career itself is an aspect of who God has called her to be. The career is not who she is. So many women have a misunderstanding of this concept. They allow their career to define who they are. These women begin to focus solely on their career, instead of their husbands and family. The family structure becomes impaired and the marriage falls apart. Strong bonds between mother and child are never made and the woman blames everyone for not understanding her career achievements. She does not recognize that she was at fault by allowing herself to not to be defined by her purpose, but by her career.

It is important that women know their career does not define them. God defines a woman's role. Your purpose defines who you are. If a woman understands the depth of this concept, she will be able to be a superwoman. She will also accomplish greatness within the corporate world, obtain academic success, and gain financial benefits. She will also understand that not only should she achieve corporate success, but marital, parental, and spiritual success. Read Proverbs 31.

Role of finances.

Is the woman the leader of the home when she makes more money than the man? The concept of being a woman with a "super-career" reflects about finances and leadership within the home. First off, let me that if you are thinking that you rule your household because you make more money, you need to check your level of pride. Pride will destroy so many things in your life if not corrected. Money in a marriage is not a prideful thing. It's not supposed to be a "my thing," rather, our thing. God said, "For this reason a man will leave his father and mother and be united to his wife, and the two will become one flesh" (Ephesians 5:31). When a woman and a man join as one through marriage, they give up their independence for dependence on each other.

They give up the "I" for us. They belong to each other and to God. Nothing in their life is to be separate. Thinking back to Ephesians 5, does God function separately from the church? If the husband displays Christ and the wife displays the church, why would they do anything separately? If everything is to be as one, why is it so hard for married couples to make their finances one too? The answers range from marrying the wrong person, someone untrustworthy, someone financial illiterate, pride, insecurity, to a poor understanding of God's plan. Review chapters 18-20.

If your marriage is to be like how God planned, your money is not to be separated when you are married. His money becomes your and vice versa. If there is a problem with that concept, then you have married the wrong person, or the wrong person married you. When marriage is built on true friendship, love, trust, and godly principles, merging money is not a matter. Contrary, when you marry outside of biblical principles, problems will arise in your marriage and be reflected in your finances. Your money will be separated and so will many other things. When a married couple has separate finances, you can best bet that other aspects of their marriage are separated too. When the money is merged, your trust in each other becomes further merged. That's what God wants—for you to further your trust in him to handle your marriage and trust in each other to make godly decisions as a unit. The way you handle money in your marriage is a big reflection of your trust level between each other.

After the finances are merged, the married couple will be able to prosper. If you are the main contributor, does that define you as the leader of the home? The answer is, no. Making more money as the woman counterpart of the marriage, does not entrust onto you the role of Adam. You are an Eve.

Not an Adam. You were made a woman, not a man. Don't waste time trying to fulfill the role of a woman and that of a man. It makes no sense to do so. If you want to play the role of a man and that of a woman, don't get married.

A man was designed to lead, and the woman was designed to support. Your finances support your marriage. Rests assure that the man you marry, no matter how much he makes, must be the provider. Don't rob him of his God-given talent. Don't turn him into wuss just because you make more money. He is to be your husband, your provider. Remember that when you get married, you can no longer operate under an independent mindset. When you do that, you fail to completely understand what marriage is about. It's not about how much you make, who makes more, and who leads in what way. It's about to people coming together to empower each other through their God-given abilities. Each partner has been given different abilities. Each person's ability is important. Don't focus too much on money, because you will lose out on the divine essence of love and marriage.

A man's role.

All this talk about a woman's role leaves me no choice but to discuss the role of a husband. This way you'll understand what type of man you should marry. The man has more responsibility on his shoulders than people tend to acknowledge. He must carry out all the God-given standards and orders as the head of the household. Read Ephesians 5:22-33. The sad part is that most men do not know the standards and orders that are from God. As a result, they fail to fulfill their role in life and marriage. Not only do men have a knowledge deficiency concerning their role, women lack insight into how a husband is supposed to function. Consequently, women choose mates unwisely.

A husband's role is to operate as Christ's masculinity in the home. This means that a man is to be the pursuer, romancer, giver, protector, leader and "savior" of his wife and family. He is to look out for the family's best interest before his very own. Think of Christ and how He fulfills our needs. Jesus sacrificed Himself to make us available to commune with Him. Placed His own life on the line was what He wanted to do to express His love for all humanity. Christ is who the husband is to display. He should place his own desires on the back burner to place God's desire in the forefront. Your husband should be leading his family in prosperity. Through his guided love, your family should follow him. As the family follows him, they follow Christ.

122

The man will make sacrifices for his family and wife, even if it will cost him his own life. The family is to admire the strength that God has given to him. He is to lead by example and his example is Christ's love and character. To his sons, he models what a man of God is like. To his daughters, he exemplifies what type of man she is to seek in a future lifetime partner. The husband is a born leader. A true leader recognizes that he must also follow. The husband's example to follow is Christ.

To his children, he is FATHER. To his wife, he is her inspiration, strength, courage, protector, provider, KING, and STRONG TOWER.

The man is the head, not the tail. Just as the woman serves as the backbone allowing the body to walk, the husband serves as the brain, sending signals to the body guiding it on how to function. The brain is one of the most fascinating organs of the body, the place where information is stored. For the brain to function properly, the host must take good care of the body. In other words, the man should be living a life that enhances who he is. Marry someone who has qualities of a leader. If you marry less than a leader, then your family will be led in the wrong direction. The brain needs the body and the body needs the brain. In unison, both the brain and spine allow the body to move and function efficiently. Otherwise, the body becomes stagnant and decayed (divorce/dysfunction/dismay).

~Role Play Challenge~

Now that we have delved into some touchy subjects, allow yourself to reflect upon what was said. I know that it's a lot to let sink in. Place the book down and take a chill pill for a few days. Over these few days ponder on the concepts. What's a woman's role? What's a man's role? The challenge is to learn your marital role. Use these biblical concepts to shape who you are and how you will function as a wife. It's up to you to have a happy marriage or an eventful divorce. Choose wisely.

~Life Scripture~

"Submit to one another out of reverence for Christ. Wives, submit yourselves to your own husbands as you do to the Lord. For the husband is the head of the wife as Christ is the head of the church, his body, of which he is the Savior.

Now as the church submits to Christ, so also wives should submit to their husbands in everything. Husbands, love your wives, just as Christ loved the church and gave himself up for her to make her holy, cleansing her by the washing with water through the word, and to present her to himself as a radiant church, without stain or wrinkle or any other blemish, but holy and blameless. In this same way, husbands ought to love their wives as their own bodies. He who loves his wife loves himself. After all, no one ever hated their own body, but they feed and care for their body, just as Christ does the church—for we are members of his body. "For this reason a man will leave his father and mother and be united to his wife, and the two will become one flesh." This is a profound mystery—but I am talking about Christ and the church. However, each one of you also must love his wife as he loves himself, and the wife must respect her husband" (Ephesians 5:21-33).

"But if serving the LORD seems undesirable to you, then choose for yourselves this day whom you will serve, whether the gods your ancestors served beyond the Euphrates, or the gods of the Amorites, in whose land you are living. But as for me and my household, we will serve the LORD" (Joshua 24:15).

~Points to Ponder~

❖ Discuss in a group what the role of a wife is, a husband, and the significance of both.

❖ What is the spiritual implication of a woman's role? Man's?

❖ Journal in your notebook how your past has shaped the way you view of submission.

❖ What are the effects of a woman controlling a man?

❖ What are the effects of marrying the wrong man?

❖ Does God call us to stay in an abusive relationship? Seek a supportive group or domestic violence counselor.

❖ Does making more money make you the leader of the home?

CHAPTER 22

WHAT PATIENCE CAN BRING

Remember my story about my failed romantic relationship, now - ships? Shortly after, I realized I didn't date within my boundaries. I dated less deserving of my qualities. Not to say that I am perfect, but as a woman of destiny, I should date a man to match my qualities. As I progressed through healing, I applied strategy number three discussed in chapter 19. I asked God, "Who should I marry?"

One day as I sat in my room, I asked God to help me write a poem about my future man. I wanted my soul to be in touch with God to poetically depict my husband. This would be the man with whom I'd share the rest of my life. As my inner being touched the heart of God, the "soul" of the pen touched paper. I expressed every thought about my future husband. His physical, spiritual, and financial well-being. I was shocked by what I wrote. Would I ever meet a man like that? Tears streamed down my face because I realized I allowed myself to date below my ideals. Why did I? Was love so farfetched in my mind that I would settle? Was I desperate and unworthy?

After re-reading what I wrote, I decided not to date until I found someone who matched my ideals more closely. Tweaking the inessentials was okay but, never the necessities. To lower my standards again to marry a man less than what I dreamt would not be an option. I asked God to give me the patience to wait to marry the right man. As a result, my poem reflected what patience can bring.

WHAT PATIENCE CAN BRING

They told me not to wait.
They said, go ahead and date.
They never understood my point of view.
I was waiting for you!
I didn't see the need to date other men,
With whom it wouldn't work back then.
I knew you would eventually come along.
My waiting time I decided to prolong.
I sought to figure out my place in life.

How I could become an excellent wife.
I enjoyed family and friends.
I rid myself of foes from back then.
As you can see now,
I found out my beauty was as awesome as the word, WOW.
My beauty went beyond skin deep.
It went to the core of my human being.
I recognized God as my maker and made Him my number one.
I did that for me, but I knew you wanted a woman with
Knowledge about where she came from.
As God and I became closer friends,
He told me what you would be.
He said you wanted a woman with God on her side.
Enough about me, let's talk about you.
Why are you smiling?
You can't believe your prayers came true?
I'm a woman blessed with brains, God, and beauty.
I see the flirting.
Stop making me blush.
I love you, but right now you should hush.
I have something to say.
As I grew into the woman before you today,
I realized what I wanted you to be.
To God be the glory, He answered every plea.
I dreamed of you being tall, brown, and handsome.
Someone I was instantly attracted to.
Not just for your outward beauty.
I saw you in so many activities.
To my understanding you were true to your Christianity.
I realized God was the center of your life.
You knew without Him you would surely die.
You treat your mother with love and respect.
Don't get me started on your intellect.
Your just like my Dad, you know all the facts.
I feel privileged to find someone smart like you.
You display your abilities by obtaining a Master's degree.
Maybe a Doctorate too.
I am proud that you waited on me.

You could have said, "I do" to someone other than me,
But you decided patience.
Now look, I met you!
Thank you for keeping your desires intact.
God knew I didn't want a man with kids running around in different homes and shacks.
My first child will also be yours.
We'll raise our family in the Lord.
Finances, you have that covered.
When you were a little boy, you decided that you'd be discovered.
Discovered for your talents and ambition.
It's weird that people think you must be poor to be Christian.
I feel financially secure with you.
I know I could stop working if I wanted to.
Love and affection, you have it all.
Whenever I need you, I can give you a call.
When times are most dear, you're always there with a prayer.
You love me to the point you've shed a tear.
I guess it's because our love is new.
One day we both will say, "I do."
Thank you for waiting on me.
Thank God for giving me patience to wait on you!

~What Patience Can Bring Challenge~

My challenge to you today is to decide to change your dating circle. Date men who meet the qualifications that are God's ideal. Never settle for love or date someone out of convenience. Don't throw in the towel on finding love. Ask God which type of characteristics you should look for in a man. Do not follow the desires of another woman, man, or even yourself. God can place these desires inside your heart. Write them in poetry format. You can also make a list. Your poem will reflect a depiction of your future husband.

~Life Scriptures~

"I waited patiently for the LORD; he turned to me and heard my cry" (Psalm 40:1).

"Stand firm, and you will win life" (Luke 21:19).

"But if we hope for what we do not yet have, we wait for it patiently" (Romans 8:25).

"Because you know that the testing of your faith produces perseverance" (James 1:3).

"Being strengthened with all power according to his glorious might so that you may have great endurance and patience" (Colossians 1:11).

"May the Lord direct your hearts into God's love and Christ's perseverance" (2 Thessalonians 3:5).

"You need to persevere so that when you have done the will of God, you will receive what he has promised" (Hebrews 10:36).

"Now faith is confidence in what we hope for and assurance about what we do not see" (Hebrews 11:1).

~Points to Ponder~

❖ Write in poetic or list format the qualities your future man should have.

❖ Define the words love and patience. How do they match?

❖ Have you ever dated below God's ideals? How did it affect your life? What did you learn?

❖ What strategy will you use to prevent yourself from settling?

❖ Discuss with friends or a book group the importance of waiting for love.

❖ Share your poem with other women in the group.

❖ Save your poem and read it on your wedding day.

❖ Has the poem come true?

❖ Read a chapter of the book of Song of Solomon as a daily devotional.

❖ Listen to "Wait for love" by Luther Vandross.

A WOMAN'S INSPIRATION FOR LIFE

CHAPTER 23

BUT, GOD

One day I looked in the mirror.
I realized that my perception was disfigured.
My pattern of thought was off kilter.
My thoughts were full of litter.
I could not see my beginning from end.
I could not see the person God called friend.
The more I stared at the mirror,
The more God began to nudge me.
The more God wanted me to see things clearer.
The more He wanted me to realize my flaws made me dearer.
Yes, I was messed up,
But God.
I was weak,
But God.
I was sinful,
But God.
I was sick,
But God.
I was weary,
But God.
I was ugly,
But God.
I was worthless,
But God.
I was all these things and more,
But God took me in and rearranged my world.
He changed my perception to that of His own.
Where I was weak,
He made me strong.
Where I was sick,
He made me whole.
Where I was sinful,
He redeemed.

Where I was worthless,
He placed value.
As I continued starring at my reflection,
All I could think was,
"I may be everything mentioned and more, but God".
As I turned to walk away from the self-reflecting mirror,
I realized that I no longer saw me.
I saw the "but God".

"And that is what some of you were. But you, were washed, you were sanctified, you were justified in the name of the Lord Jesus Christ and by the Spirit of our God" (1 Corinthians 6:11).

~But, God Challenge~

Today's challenge is for you to realize that your entire life, you allowed negative thoughts to occupy your mind, negatively impact your life, and determine what you think about yourself. You have allowed negativity take over. The wrongful thing(s) he or she did to you shaped the way you think. It has caused you to forget the "but God's" in your life. You may have fallen, but you can get back up again. You may not like yourself, but you can learn to love yourself again. You may have lost your way, but you can be found again.

Don't forget the but's. Life can only shape us the way we allow. It is about our perspective of our circumstances. Do we choose to take away the positive and leave the negative? Do we take the negative and leave the positive? This is what determines our perception. How you view each situation will create an atmosphere of positivity or negativity. Choose today to release the negative and embrace the positive. Remember the "but's".

~Life Scriptures~

"You intended to harm me, but God intended it for good to accomplish what is now being done, the saving of many lives" (Genesis 50:20).

"David stayed in the wilderness strongholds and in the hills of the Desert of Ziph. Day after day Saul searched for him, but God did not give David into his hands" (1 Samuel 23:14).

"My flesh and my heart may fail, but God is the strength of my heart and my portion forever" (Psalm 73:26).

"Once you were not a people, but now you are the people of God; once you had not received mercy, but now you have received mercy" (1 Peter 2:10).

~Points to Ponder~

- ❖ What negative words have you allowed to define you?
- ❖ Define the word negativity. How is it different from positivity?
- ❖ What are some ways that you can incorporate positive thinking, people, and situations into your life?
- ❖ How can speaking negatively affect your life?

Chapter 24

Happy being Me

I'm so happy being me.
Happy living life freely.
No more compromise.
No more lavish lies.
I am so happy being me.
Happy living life freely.
Happy to run.
Happy to soar.
I am so happy being me.
Happy living life freely.
No more doubts.
No more of life's droughts.
I am so happy being me.
Happy living life freely.
Happy to live.
Happy to give.
I am so happy being me.
Happy living life freely.
No more thinking.
No more wishing.
I am so happy being me.
Happy living life freely.
Happy looking forward.
Happy being groomed by the Lord.
I am so happy being me.
Happy living life freely.
No looking back.
No more of life's cracks.
I am so happy being me.
Happy living life freely.
Happy to learn.
Happy to grow.
Happy to love.
Happy to sow.

No more mistakes.
No more heartbreaks.
No more misuse.
No more blues.
I am so happy being me.
Happy living life freely.

~Happy Being Me Challenge~

The purpose of this book was to allow you to see the woman God created you to be. I want you to be happy simply being yourself! If you can't be happy being you, then who will be happy for you? No one can bring you happiness, except God. God is a necessity for the lives of all women. God is the one who can bring us joy. God always desires us to play a vital part in this process.

He uses us in intricate ways to bring joy to our lives. He will give us a purpose, talents, friends, employment, and so on, for us to use these things to experience happiness. Where does happiness begin? It begins in a founded relationship with God. It's time ladies. It's time to arise and look for the vision that God has given you. It's time to acknowledge what God has given you which is the ability to stand up and be happy being you!

~Life Scripture~

"I have told you this so that my joy may be in you and that your joy may be complete" (John 15:11).

"You have given me greater joy than those who have abundant harvests of grain and new wine" (Psalm 4:7).

"Yet I will rejoice in the Lord! I will be joyful in the God of my salvation" (Habakkuk 3:18).

"The Lord is my strength and my shield; my heart trusts in Him, and He helps me. My heart leaps for joy, and with my song I praise Him" (Psalm 28:7).

"For God so loved the world that he gave his one and only Son, that whoever believes in him shall not perish but have eternal life. For God did not send his

Son into the world to condemn the world, but to save the world through him. Whoever believes in him is not condemned, but whoever does not believe stands condemned already because he has not believed in the name of God's one and only Son" (John 3:16-18).

~Points to Ponder~

❖ Define the words happiness, self-confidence, and contentment.

❖ Which Bible passages talk about these words?

❖ Are you a happy woman? Why or why not?

❖ What have you learned throughout this journey? Write what you discovered in your note pad. Maybe share your journey with another woman.

❖ List 3 key points God is teaching you about your life.

❖ List 3 life goals and discuss how you are going to accomplish them.

❖ This week listen to the song, "So Happy Being Me" by Donald Lawrence or Angie Stone. Make this song you theme song for the week. Allow the lyrics to give you motivation to be happy being you.

CHAPTER 25

MOTIVATIONAL & INSPIRATIONAL QUOTES

"There's nothing like being romanced and the greatest romance is with the One who created me." – Stephanneth Adams

"And we know that in all things God works for the good of those who love him, who have been called according to his purpose" (Romans 8:28).

"Every person placed in our life is a blessing from God. The objective is to figure out why they are there. In each circumstance there is a lesson learned and a blessing gained. Don't hate the season because all seasons change. Change is good so the next season can enter!" – Stephanneth Adams

"When we function in our purpose, we become an asset and not a liability to other people. God can use us the way He made us." – Stephanneth Adams

"Now faith is being sure of what we hope for and certain of what we do not see" (Hebrews 11:1).

"God is the first man you need in your life. Always make your earthly man number two!"- Stephanneth Adams

"No weapon forged against you will prevail, and you will refute every tongue that accuses you" (Isaiah 54:17).

"Don't believe a liar because they lie."- Anonymous

"Until you understand your personality type and who you are, you will not function effectively in the world." – Stephanneth Adams

"A wife of noble character who can find? She is worth far more than rubies. Her husband has full confidence in her and lacks nothing of value" (Proverbs 31:10-11).

"How do you think the both of you will last forever when God is not in the center of your love? Re-think your strategy!" – Stephanneth Adams

"Love is having the attitude of stick-to-itiveness when times get hard." - Stephanneth Adams

"And I will do whatever you ask in my name, so that the Son may bring glory to the Father. You may ask me for anything in my name, and I will do it" (John 14:13-14).

"Like a ruby, I wait for that miner who is willing to get his shovel from God and dig through solid ground to find me, his wife!" –Stephanneth Adams

"He thinks I am something! Who you ask? God!" – Stephanneth Adams

"Therefore I tell you, whatever you ask for in prayer, believe that you have received it, and it will be yours" (Mark 11:24).

"Sometimes love includes loving who you are first, or should that always be?"-Stephanneth Adams

"In the midst of life's troubles, you have to be strong when you feel weak." - Stephanneth Adams

"Therefore, I urge you, brothers, in view of God's mercy, to offer your bodies as living sacrifices, holy and pleasing to God-this is your spiritual act of worship. Do not conform any longer to the pattern of this world, but be transformed by the renewing of your mind. Then you will be able to test and approve what God's will is—his good, pleasing and perfect will" (Romans 12:1-2).

"Even when you are physically blind have a supernatural vision." - Stephanneth Adams

"But your hearts must be fully committed to the Lord our God, to live by his decrees and obey his commands, as at this time" (I Kings 8:61).

"Girl if he left you, trust me, his amnesia will wear off." - Stephanneth Adams

"The Lord is my light and my salvation whom shall I fear? The Lord is the stronghold of my life of whom shall I be afraid? When evil men advance against me to devour my flesh, when my enemies and my foes attack me, they will stumble and fall. Though an army besiege me, my heart will not fear; though war break out against me, even then will I be confident" (Psalm 27:1-3).

"Sometimes love means letting go even though it's hard." - Stephanneth Adams

"Be diligent in these matters; give yourself wholly to them, so that everyone may see your progress" (1 Timothy 4:15).

"I want forever lasting love, not forever temporary." – Stephanneth Adams

"So watch yourselves. If your brother sins, rebuke him, and if he repents, forgive him. If he sins against you seven times in a day, and seven times comes back to you and says, 'I repent,' forgive him" (Luke 17:3-4).

"Before I formed you in the womb I knew you, before you were born I set you apart; I appointed you as a prophet to the nations" (Jeremiah 1:5).

"Trust in the Lord and do good; dwell in the land and enjoy safe pasture. Delight yourself in the Lord and he will give you the desires of your heart" (Psalm 37:3-4).

"Instead of possessing the power to blow up, possess the power to remain calm." - Stephanneth Adams

"If you place God in the mix of your life, your life batter will taste much sweeter." - Stephanneth Adams

"Sorry, you're not on my EDD (Expected Date of Delivery) list. Try again!" - Stephanneth Adams

"Your passion should be your career and your career your passion." - Stephanneth Adams

"Going through the trials of life allows my human flesh to die, makes me a new person, and impregnates me with destiny." - Stephanneth Adams

"Single ladies stop dating triple L men: lost, lazy, and ludicrous. Date triple G men: godly, great, and gentlemen. Otherwise, remain a triple S woman: single, saved, and satisfied." - Stephanneth Adams

"If he knew what he had, he would've hitched me to his side like Velcro. Instead, he was too blind to see that he had me in his hand like quicksand!" – Stephanneth Adams

"By the time you get your life together, my eggs will have hatched and another rooster in the coop." – Stephanneth Adams

~Points to Ponder~

❖ Share one of these quotes in-person or on social media with a woman who may need it.
❖ Write some of your favorite quotes and scriptures in your note pad.
❖ Create a few personal quotes and share them to your social media page. Inspire someone else.

CHAPTER 26

DEPARTING WORDS WOMAN TO WOMAN

Dear sister, we have come to the end of our journey, but not the end of your life. Together we have confessed our sins, owned our mistakes, experienced pain, and shared our stories. Most of all, we have experienced the freedom and joy that comes from being delivered from our problems, sins, pain, and past. We have experienced God's forgiveness, compassion, wisdom, and love. Through each chapter God's love has poured into our souls. Now, we walk with a purpose. We now know our destiny. Most of all, we know why we were created.

Thank you for taking your time to travel this journey with me. I hope that you were inspired and understood the provided biblical-based wisdom. I know that God has a specific destiny in mind just for you. This is the reason why you were led to read this book. Don't forget that Life's Journey: Woman to Woman didn't fall into your hands by happenstance. This book was divinely placed into your hands, whether to deliver you from the pain of your past or propel you into a bright future. This book was meant for you. Take every word, chapter, revelation, and comfort to heart for the rest of your life's journey.

I look forward to hearing from you. It is my desire to know how your life has been transformed and renewed by reading this book. Please send your questions, comments, testimonies, or prayer request to lifesjourney_w2w@yahoo.com. Remember that life is a journey. The roads we choose during this journey may lead us to a sad or happy ending. Be mindful of the path you choose to walk. Continue to walk in the goodness of God.

1 John 1:7 says, "But if we walk in the light, as he is in the light, we have fellowship with one another, and the blood of Jesus, his Son, purifies us from all sin."

MEET THE AUTHOR

Dr. Stephanneth Adams is the author of Life's Journey: Woman to Woman, a woman's devotional workbook. She loves to address the issues of a woman's soul. Her passion is to help women which is why she became a Doctor of Nursing Practice with a specialty in Women's Health. Through her studies she learned the physiological and social needs of women. Being a woman herself, she understands that women struggle with varying issues. Through her faith, teachings of God's principles, and women's health studies, she has learned basic principles that can help any woman overcome her life's obstacles. These teachings also help women to build a foundation for a bright future. It's inspiration for the woman's soul!

She was born in Tacoma Park, Maryland to the proud parents of Dr. Stenneth and Mrs. Stephanie Adams. She was reared in a home where God, education, love, and respect were strongly valued. Through these same principles, she learned tips that could guide her along her life's journey. As most young women do, she found herself not listening to wisdom and seeking guidance on her own terms. Pitfalls have popped up here and there, but with God she has been able to remain spiritually focused and goal oriented. These are principles she desires all women to obtain.

Giving her life to Christ at the age of 17 is something she never regrets. Faith and hope have led her to become the woman she was created to be. Faith and hope gave her the words to say to all women, "It gets better than this. All you have to do is trust in God's supernatural power." What was her purpose of writing this book? The purpose was to bring healing to the hurting woman, hope to the hopeless woman, and wisdom to the questioning woman. The book is a source of inspiration for any woman journeying through life.

Don't miss out on your source of inspiration!
Share it your girlfriends, mother, neighbors, first lady, or grandma, to inspire them too!

Email: lifesjourney_w2w@yahoo.com
Instagram: @transformativebbj
Podcasts: www.blogtalkradio.com/lifesjourney

My Note Pad

184

WRITE THE VISION. MAKE IT PLAIN.

(Habakkuk 2:2)

Made in the USA
Las Vegas, NV
19 March 2022

45922225R00115